Models of Collaboration

MODELS OF COLLABORATION

Mary Susan E. Fishbaugh
Montana State University—Billings

Allyn and Bacon
Boston • London • Toronto • Sydney • Tokyo • Singapore

Vice President, Education: Nancy Forsyth
Series Editor: Ray Short
Editorial Assistant: Christine Svitila
Marketing Manager: Kris Farnsworth
Editorial-Production Service: Shepherd, Inc.
Composition and Prepress Buyer: Linda Cox
Manufacturing Buyer: Suzanne Lareau
Cover Administrator: Suzanne Harbison

Library of Congress Cataloging-in-Publication Data

Fishbaugh, Mary Susan.
  Models of collaboration / Mary Susan E. Fishbaugh.
      p.   cm.
  Includes bibliographical references and index.
  ISBN 0–205–18441–3
  1. Teaching teams—United States. 2. Mentoring in education—United States
  3. Master teachers—United States.   I. Title.
  LB1029.T4F57   1996
  371.148—dc20   96–41881
                                                                                CIP

Printed in the United States of America
10 9 8 7 6 5 4 3 2 1   00 99 98 97 96

To the Holy Spirit

CONTENTS

FOREWORD

In 1971, a year after graduating from the University of California at Santa Barbara with a bachelor of arts degree in political science, I joined a college friend in Salt Lake City, Utah. The "rational" purpose of this journey was to work in a summer camp sponsored by United Cerebral Palsy of Utah. The fact that I had no experience working with individuals with disabilities made no difference at all. I had three things going for me: I had a college degree, I was available, and my friend was the camp director.

When the camp ended six weeks later, my life had changed. I started the camp having had literally no contact with individuals with disabilities for 22 years and ended it with 40 new friends, some who had very significant multiple disabilities. Flushed with discovery, I set about looking for employment in the disability field. Somewhat to my surprise, I was successful. Even though there was not yet an *Education of the Handicapped Act* (EHA), the State of Utah had been persuaded by litigation to provide a free public education to children and youth with disabilities. However, there were no strict regulations on hiring special educators with teaching certificates, so, as a college graduate, I was a marketable individual.

When my teaching career in special education began, I knew one thing very well: I didn't have a clue on how to teach anything to anyone. So, the students with disabilities that I worked with were at no more of a disadvantage than any other student would have been. What I did know is that I needed help and I wasn't afraid to ask for it. Thus, began my first experience in collaborating with others in the education of individuals with disabilities. Believe me, we needed one another because there weren't many of us who actually had a special education teaching certificate.

Five years later, I found myself in a masters degree program at the University of Utah which included courses for a special education teaching certificate (category: intellectually handicapped). At the time, I didn't realize the significance of what the faculty were saying about those of us in the first cohort to be prepared to teach according to the EHA (P.L. 94-142). I do know that we were schooled from day one on the components of an IEP and how to write one. As much as I appreciated the program and the faculty, I kept hearing variations on a theme. Along the way, I learned Deno's (1970) Cascade of Services, the continuum of least restrictive environment, and the concept of mainstreaming.* When I graduated from the program two years later, I felt fully prepared to teach children with disabilities.

Like most first year teachers, my reality check came in the first month on the job. Between teaching groups of students, conducting assessments on students referred to special education, participating in IEP meetings, and writing IEPs, I found myself awash in the work of special education. I was so busy, I didn't even notice the sideward glances of the veteran elementary education teachers in the school building.

By December, I began to observe the glances of these teachers and realized that I had done very little in the way of talking with them about "their students" in "my resource room." With referrals and testing slowing down, I began to use more time to talk with the teams of elementary education teachers. I listened to their observations of the special education students in their classrooms, and I occasionally observed some of these students in their regular classrooms. Of the latter, I learned some startling things: the behavior of some children varied widely from the regular classroom to the resource room, almost in opposite. A few students who could barely stop talking in my groups were reserved to withdrawn in their regular classrooms. A few others who were sullenly quiet in the resource room exhibited an optimistic confidence even though their academic performance was generally lower than that of other students. Clearly, the grade level teachers, my co-special education teacher, and I had much to discuss about "the resource room kids."

Without any fanfare, we special education teachers and general education teachers began to regularly *consult* and *collaborate* on everything from curriculum materials and instructional methods to behavior management. Our goal was to make the schooling of students with disabilities more cohesive through our mutual efforts as teachers. Some teachers actually brought their entire classes of students into the resource room and we rotated groups through a series of instructional activities. Sometimes, my colleague and I would go to regular classrooms and do the same.

*Deno, E. (1970). "Special education as developmental capital." *Exceptional Children* 37: 229–237.

Not surprisingly, much of our collaborative efforts were trial and error with only passive support from the principal and district administration. But when spring parent conferences came around we were pleasantly surprised to find that several parents mentioned how much they appreciated our approach to keeping their children with their classmates in their homerooms. The experience was very gratifying for us as teachers, but the benefits for children were amazing. When we analyzed the results of the ritualistic spring testing, we found that students in the resource program made significant gains beyond any other previous year.

This bit of personal history came back to me as I read Mary Susan Fishbaugh's text. How great it would have been to have such a resource in my teacher education program and as a teacher. Much of our initial efforts at collaboration would have undoubtedly gone smoother, and student performance would likely have been even better had we started our collaboration from day one. Fortunately, current and future teachers now have access to this book, *Models of Collaboration*. Some individuals will say that teachers already have more than enough to learn without adding collaboration to the list. Mary Susan Fishbaugh will convince you that working collaboratively for the education of our children is the overarching framework from which all teaching and learning takes place.

Ernest Rose Ph.D.
Dean, College of Education and Human Services
Montana State University—Billings

PREFACE

Models of Collaboration has been written to begin building a theory of professional collaboration. The book has grown from years of reading about collaboration, working collaboratively in elementary and secondary public schools, and teaching undergraduate and graduate students about collaborative practice. Teaching about something is the best way to fully understand it. As I continued to read about, work in, and teach collaboration, I became frustrated with the many definitions of the term, the artificial distinction made between consultation and collaboration, and the potential semantic arguments that could arise from the professional literature on collaboration. The resources available for teaching collaboration courses provided excellent information and training with regard to specific skills needed, but lacked a common framework for basic understanding. The purpose of this book is to begin building that common basis.

I began my professional career in general elementary education, but quickly realized that the primary aged children who were in my "readiness" class were not a homogeneous lot. Each child had individual strengths and individual needs. As I moved into administrative positions and participated in IEP meetings, I came to understand the similarities among students. Those who qualified as students needing special education services were not so different from those who did not qualify according to state and federal guidelines. How could individual teachers, working alone in a classroom, hope to meet the varied needs of fifteen to thirty students? How could one person teach to the academically gifted student, the "average" (Is there really such a person?) child, and the students with special educational needs whether or not they qualified for special services? These questions remain valid today. Collaborative practice, working together for a common end, is one answer.

I am hoping that *Models of Collaboration* will initiate debate on the definition of professional collaboration. Although written from the perspective of a life long educator, the book applies to other professions as well. The continuum of consulting, coaching, and teaming models can be discerned anywhere that there is a need for professional interaction in order to get the job done. Professional debate on the models as developed in this book will clarify the meaning of collaborative practice, and in so doing, will guide professionals as they strive to improve their collaborative efforts.

I would like to acknowledge those who have supported me in this endeavor. James Ruppel, Allyn & Bacon's Publisher's Representative, encouraged me to submit a prospectus. Ray Short, my editor, was willing to gamble on a novice author. Mike and Jo Jakupcak, my friends and professional colleagues at the University of Montana in Missoula, read early drafts of the manuscript and were willing to pilot them in classes. I am very appreciative of my students who over the course of several semesters put up with the lack of a text, endured the frustration of having their text on reserve, but provided me with constructive criticism nonetheless.

I look forward to response to this book and I hope that my readers will take the time to share their opinions with me.

Mary Susan E. Fishbaugh, Ed.D.
Director of Professional Practices
Montana State University—Billings
August, 1996

1

INTRODUCTION

Vignette

Sarah taught for fifteen years in Blue Spruce, Montana. Blue Spruce is a small community in the northeastern corner of the state on the high line. Surrounded by the prairie that has been tamed into vast fields of golden wheat, Blue Spruce is only thirty miles from the Canadian border. The town boasts fifty families, the requisite bar, post office, and of course a school. Blue Spruce School is the heart of the town. High school sports, especially basketball, constitute the only winter recreational opportunities. Winters are long and cold on the high line with subzero temperatures for weeks on end, arctic wind chills swooping down from Canada, long nights and short days. From November through March, and sometimes April, the rolling wheat fields are hidden by several feet of snow. Most days it is difficult to distinguish earth from sky as they blend into a frozen white horizon. Sarah loved the open ruggedness of eastern Montana, and she loved her position as the only special education teacher at Blue Spruce School. It is a K–12 school with a multicultural student body numbering approximately 125 students. Although Sarah's caseload averaged only twenty students per year, her responsibilities were sometimes overwhelming. Not only did she implement the students' IEP's, but she consulted with general education teachers, coordinated post school rehabilitation services, and counseled parents, all in the name of her position as a special education teacher. After fifteen years, Sarah decided to request a professional leave in order to earn her master of special education degree at an in-state university. Her program of study has emphasized the need for coordination, cooperation, and collaboration among professionals working with students, either in school or through community agencies. With the background of her own teaching experience, Sarah viewed this emphasis as less than profound, however, she quickly became confused with the proliferation of collaborative examples. As the time

to face the literature review for her thesis approached, Sarah pondered over orga-
nizing, analyzing, and evaluating the many "models" of collaborative practice.

Chapter Outline

Vignette

Chapter Outline

Chapter Content

      Purpose of Models of Collaboration
      Evolution of Collaborative Practice in Education
         and the Human Services
      Overview of Subsequent Chapters
      Collaboration Portfolio Development through Chapter Activities
         The Purpose of Student Portfolio Development
         The Value of Action Research

Summary

Vignette Reprise

Portfolio Activities

References

PURPOSE OF *MODELS OF COLLABORATION*

The purpose for a text on models of collaboration is to provide a frame-work for collaborative practice among professionals in education and the human services. Although the word "collaboration" is frequently used in educational professional literature, there has not been a consensus on its definition. Idol, Paolucci-Whitcomb, and Nevin (1987; 1994) describe collaborative consultation. Morsink, Thomas, and Correa (1991) explain interactive teaming. West, Idol, and Cannon (1989) have produced a practical guide for school collaboration. Pugach and Johnson (1995) discuss collaborative school practice. Welch and Sheridan (1995) write about educational partnerships for students who are at risk. Authors assume a common understanding of collaborative practice in educational settings. While the collaborative practices described have similarities, they also differ in some ways. *Models of Collaboration* has been written to provide a structure for thinking about collaborative practice.

The history of education in the United States demonstrates that early public schooling was a one-man show. Teachers were responsible for the group of students in their own classrooms. Envision the public or private school of a century ago—a stark room with desks in straight rows, facing one end of the room where the teacher's desk was front-and-center. The teacher stood at a blackboard or sat at his (the teacher was often a man) desk facing the students to "teach." The teacher was synonymous with authority in the classroom and the teaching involved lecturing to or demonstrating for the students. In small rural communities, such as Blue Spruce, the school may have been only one room, a situation exacerbating the control and isolation of an individual teacher.

Because society was agriculturally based, students who didn't do well in school quit. They had the option of working the land, ranching, or riding the frontier. Although there may have been a range of ability in any one class, students whose aptitudes were not academic need not continue. They did not have to stay in school until they were sixteen years old. They did not need a high school diploma or post high school training to farm. Because societal mores were simpler, students knew the behavioral expectations of their student role. Although there may have been mischievous students who were considered to be "problems" by their teachers, there were not the number and magnitude of inappropriate behaviors as exhibited in today's classrooms. If students did not comply with the authority vested in the teacher, they could be expelled.

Society has changed. This country has evolved from an agrarian culture through the industrial revolution to a highly complex technologically based economy. With this change has come the need for more education and increasingly specialized training. Students must stay in school longer and must be literate in many areas in order to compete for employment as young adults. As society has become more complex, traditional values have been questioned. The social revolution of the "baby boomers" during the decade of the 1960s that called into question the validity of "the establishment" foreshadowed the uncertainty and seeming lack of direction experienced by today's youth. Because society has changed, so must the schools change as social institutions.

Gone are the days of an individual teacher in a classroom behind a closed door. No longer can one person hope to meet the many, varied, and unusual needs of a classroom of thirty students. By working together, teachers can share their expertise and can share the burden of responsibility for overall student outcomes. Such teaming has been federally mandated by the Individuals with Disabilities Education Act (IDEA, 1990). This special education law demands that a multidisciplinary team of people assess a student's strengths and needs, then meet together in order to develop an individualized education program (IEP) for the student. Such teaming is required by Section 504 of the Rehabilitation Act of 1973. Subpart D of Section 504 addresses nondiscrimination on the basis of disability or perceived disability in preschool, elementary, and secondary education. With an emphasis on the responsibilities of regular educators, this law states that a group of people knowledgeable about the child, the tests used for assessment, and the school's resources work together to develop a general education intervention plan for the student. The multidisciplinary team or group includes participation from educationally related areas such as mental health professionals, rehabilitation counselors, educational psychologists and social workers, parents, and any other professional or paraprofessional who may have insight into an individual student's educational needs.

Both special education enabling legislation (IDEA) and civil rights nondiscriminatory legislation (Section 504) mandate that students have a right to a free and appropriate public education (FAPE) in the least restrictive environment (LRE). The inclusion of students with special educational needs in general education classrooms requires a team approach to educational programming. A single teacher cannot effectively teach a class of students with a wide range of academic abilities and a wider range of aptitudes and interests. Increasing diversity in the general education program demands collaboration among teachers, classroom assistants, and other support personnel. Increasingly diverse student needs demand collaboration beyond the schoolhouse door. Educators must collaborate with professionals in other human service agencies in order to meet the educational needs of their students. While educational collaboration will maintain the overriding goal of successful educational outcomes for each student, the form that the collaborative practice takes may vary. Sometimes a consultant may be enlisted for advice about student programming, similar to the consultation described by Idol et al. (1987; 1994). Sometimes teachers coach each other through the initial phases of implementing new teaching methods in a manner similar to peer clinical supervision (McFaul and Cooper, 1984). At other times, a team of people may meet to seek a solution to an immediate educational dilemma as envisioned by Morsink et al. (1991).

To be most effective, educators should have a theoretical structure on which they can base their collaboration. Collaboration means working together for a common end. As educators and human services professionals collaborate, they should do so with a knowledge of different models for collaborating, and recognition of the different purposes for their collaborative practice. With a framework for collaboration, an understanding of this structure, and reflection as to purpose, professionals will be more effective in their collaborative efforts. They will be better prepared to choose the appropriate model for a specific purpose, analyze their use of the model, and evaluate their collaboration. *Models of Collaboration* proposes such a structure.

In this text, educational collaboration is described according to three models—consulting, coaching, and teaming (see Figure 1.1). Although distinguishable, the three approaches can blend into each other. Theoretically, each is defined and discussed as if it were a discrete entity. Practice is never quite so clear cut as theory, so examples of these three basic models may exhibit aspects of more than one of the models, or may combine model use. In addition, the text proposes three basic purposes for any collaborative effort—technical assistance, collegial support, or challenge solution (Garmston, 1987). The overriding goal of collaborative practice is student achievement; but in order to reach that goal, collaboration may be used to provide technical assistance to teachers as they work with students or as they practice new techniques. Collaboration may be employed to provide support among teachers as they work with especially difficult students or as they strive for personal professional development. Collaboration among educators may be necessary for solving immediate or long-range individual student or school-wide challenges. *Models of Collaboration* attempts to provide an explanation of these three proposed basic collaborative models and to facilitate an understanding of how they can be employed to achieve the three basic purposes of collaborative practice. Gaining understanding of collaboration and reflecting on its purposes will ensure more effective collaborative practice.

Consulting (Expert)

The consulting model of collaboration is defined by inequality. An expert gives advice to a person less knowledgable in the consultant's field of expertise. In the consulting model, information flows one way, from the consultant to the consultee.

Coaching (Parity)

The coaching model of collaboration is defined by parity. Two or more people take turns advising each other. In the coaching model, information flows two ways, but this two-way directional flow does not occur simultaneously.

Teaming (Interactive)

The teaming model of collaboration is defined by interaction. All members of the team have equal ownership of team problems and solutions. In the teaming model, information flows in several directions at once, from one member to the others, as different members assume leadership or follower roles dictated by situational needs.

FIGURE 1.1 **Models of Collaboration**

EVOLUTION OF COLLABORATIVE PRACTICE
IN EDUCATION AND THE HUMAN SERVICES

Cook and Friend (1991) have briefly traced the evolution of collaborative practice in education and the human services. Consultation is defined as a process through which one professional assists another in solving a problem concerning a third person. Consultation began in the social services during the early twentieth century when large numbers of European immigrants required help from agencies not adequately staffed to meet the demand. The consultative approach in education began in the mid-seventies with the passage of P.L. 94-142. This indirect service delivery model was necessary to meet the demand for special education service delivery in the absence of needed, adequately trained special education teachers.

As a consultant, a special educator served as a resource to general education teachers. An early text by Wiederholt, Hammill, and Brown (1983) guided preparation of resource room teachers. In such a role the teacher is expected to maintain a caseload of students who are seen on a regular basis, but the teacher also serves as a classroom consultant to other teachers working with the same students and with others who demonstrate similar educational needs. Sugai and Tindal (1993) have provided a behavioral approach to consultation. The educational consultant's role has been elaborated upon by Heron and Harris (1993), as well as by Idol (1993) in handbooks for consultants.

Cook and Friend (1991) distinguish consultation from collaboration. In contrast to the unequal relationship of persons involved in a consulting model, collaboration involves interaction between two or more equal parties who voluntarily share decision making in working toward a common goal. This definition of collaboration is actually interactive teaming as described by Morsink, Thomas, and Correa (1991) or collaborative consultation as described by Idol, Nevin, and Paolucci-Whitcomb (1994) in the second edition of their text by the same name. In contrast, *Models of Collaboration* presents a framework in which consultation and teaming are presented as different forms of collaboration.

Cook and Friend (1991) envision the future of collaboration as a way to meet the needs of individuals in a complex society. They propose including the client in decision making. They project a growing need for collaboration among service providers and agencies in meeting the multiple service needs of clients.

Johnson, Pugach, and Devlin (1990) describe the history of educational collaboration as a progressive movement from the prescriptive nature of consultation to the mutual parity of collaboration. They present six steps for developing a more collaborative educational environment:

- Sanctioning of collaborative efforts by administration
- Providing assistance for teachers with clerical work and other non-instructional tasks
- Organizing meeting times for teachers to engage in mutual problem solving
- Providing opportunities for specialists and teachers to co-teach
- Developing common vocabulary and terminology in order to avoid specialized jargon
- Reserving regular faculty or in-service meetings for collaboration

As will be seen in later chapters, these suggestions are echoed by others who write about educational collaboration. In *Models of Collaboration,* consultation is not viewed as less progressive than is collaboration, but as a different form. The prescriptions of a consultant are often necessary before a mutual level of professional expertise between or among collaborators has developed. Consultation is not viewed as non-collaborative, but is presented as a form of collaboration defined by expertise on the part of one collaborator and the need for that expertise on the part of another. The six steps for developing a collaborative environment apply to the consulting approach just as they apply to a teaming approach in which collaborators work from a more equal basis.

With the passage of P.L. 99-457 (1986) and mandated provision of educational services at an earlier age, collaboration has been dubbed the sine qua non of successful integration for young children. Hanson and Widerstrom (1992) define consultation as a process of giving advice, and collaboration as a different type of helping relationship involving equality of those participating. They state that interagency collaboration is an essential ingredient for successful preschool special education programs and describe several exemplary programs. The following recommendations for effective consultation and collaboration include elements similar to those proposed by Johnson et al. (1990):

- Commitment from decision makers
- Commitment, shared ownership, and decision making among participants
- Adequate resources to support planning and coordination
- Ongoing training and technical assistance
- Evaluation
- Family involvement

These authors distinguish collaboration from consultation in a fashion similar to that described earlier. Again, this separation of consultation from collaboration is viewed as artificial in this text. Consultation is a form of collaboration for which commitment from all involved parties, adequate resources, ongoing technical assistance, and evaluation are important components for success of the collaborative effort. Just as Cook and Friend (1991) envision an increasing need for collaboration among service providers, and as Hanson and Widerstrom (1992) suggest family involvement in educational collaboration, *Models of Collaboration* has been written with the philosophy that consulting, coaching, and teaming apply across human service agencies.

Educators and other human services professionals collaborate in a variety of ways as suggested by Voltz (1993). They routinely exchange information about student progress, coordinate development of instructional plans, team teach, plan for generalization of skills, jointly conduct parent conferences, share decisions with regard to grades, collaboratively problem solve, and participate in cooperative professional development.

Educational collaboration has been termed a catalyst for change in an article by Idol and West (1991) that provides a potpourri of information. They define collaboration as an interactive relationship, an adult-to-adult interactive process. The authors suggest an eight-step process for collaboration involving goal setting, data collection, problem identification, development of alternative solutions, action plan development, action plan implementation, evaluation, and redesign. They list thirteen principles for collaborative consultation that include establishing team member relationships, respect among the team, use of situational leadership, conflict management, information sharing, active listening, nonjudgmental responding, interviewing skills, common language, data gathering, willingness to receive as well as give feedback, giving credit where credit is due, and awareness of nonverbal messages. A collaborative school is based on norms of collegiality, the professionalization of teaching, a wide array of practices, and shared decision making among all staff with the overriding goal of educational improvement. Facilitative strategies involve administrative leadership supporting time for collaboration and commitment to ongoing professional development. Ways to build a collaborative school structure include site-based decision making, empowering committees of educational professionals, developing departmental or grade-level instructional teams, and developing teacher assistance teams. These authors stress the importance of administrative commitment to and support of collaborative efforts in order to ensure success.

The relationship of collaboration to change is viewed as interactive in this book. On the one hand, collaborative practice is a change in the way schools do business. On the other hand, awareness of the components of successful change efforts mirrors supports necessary for educational collaboration and can preclude unnecessary conflict in collaborative practice.

The steps to collaboration as delineated by Idol and West (1991) that include goal setting, data collection, evaluation, and redesign, correspond to the components of clinical supervision as formulated by Cogan (1973). Developed as an antidote to routinized, summative teacher appraisals, clinical supervision involves a five-step process: preconference, observation and data collection, data analysis, postconference, and self-reflection (see Figure 1.2). The purpose of clinical supervision is continual teacher professional development in a nonthreatening environment. The purposes of collaboration involve technical improvement to promote student growth, collegial support for professional development, or collaborative problem solving. Because clinical supervision is compatible in both process and philosophy with collaborative practice, the process can be used as a basic tool in each of the three collaboration models.

Preconference

Observer and observed meet to clarify needed assistance/professional interest/challenge, to determine the focus of an observation, and the method of data collection.

Although the above activities should lead to mutually agreed upon decisions, the meetings should be driven by the needs of the person to be observed.

Observation and Data Collection

Observer collects requested data according to the method agreed upon during the preconference.

Data Analysis

Observer and observed each analyze and interpret resulting data.

Postconference

Observer and observed meet to discuss their individual perceptions of the observation data and to determine future action based on data analysis.

Self-Reflection

Observer evaluates his/her ability to be a facilitator of the observed's data analysis and problem solutions. The Observer's role is to empower the observed, rather than to analyze the data and solve the problem him/herself.

FIGURE 1.2   Clinical Observation

When a consultant is called to assist with a student problem, an introductory visit may be scheduled for problem clarification (preconference). The consultant usually requests time with the student, either as an observer or as a participant observer in the classroom (observation). The consultant will then review notes (data analysis) and discuss with the teacher possible strategies for use with the student (postconference). The consultant may request an evaluation of their work from the school (self-reflection).

Similarly, coaching uses the clinical supervision cycle. As teachers coach each other for their mutual professional development, they will first meet to determine personal professional goals and to decide on the focus of an in-class observation (preconference). One of them will then observe in the classroom of the other (observation). After the observation, both teachers look at the observation notes (data analysis) and meet again to discuss possible changes in teaching strategies and future observation dates (postconference). The observer may request feedback from the observed teacher with regard to the observer's role as facilitator of data analysis and coach for professional change (self-reflection).

Teacher assistance teams or prereferral teams (see Chapter 6, "Teaming") are frequently used in schools before formal referral of a student to special education. A group of people, usually including several teachers, an administrator, a related services person, and a classroom assistant meet to discuss a student at risk of school failure (preconference). One or all of the team members agree to observe the student in one or more settings (observation). The team meets again to discuss the observation(s) (data analysis), to brainstorm possible strategies for use with the student, and to determine means for evaluating success of their efforts (postconference). The team may ask the teacher of the at-risk student to assess their effectiveness in addressing the teacher's concerns about the student (self-reflection).

Peer clinical supervision (McFaul and Cooper, 1984) is a form of peer coaching that has been employed for technical assistance and improvement. Peer coaching has been espoused by Joyce and Weil (1986) as a means of support for teachers who are practicing a new model of teaching. Peer supervision/coaching has been used in the Program for Effective Teaching (PET) developed by Madeline Hunter (Mandeville and Rivers, 1989). Through coaching teachers helped one another perfect implementation of Hunter's lesson design. For application to collaborative practice, the clinical supervision process is being renamed clinical "observation" to offset the negative connotations of the word "supervision." The integrity of the clinical process, however, remains intact.

The principles listed by Idol and West (1991) can be compared to principles of developmental supervision as described by Glickman (1990; Glickman, Gordon, and Ross-Gordon, 1995). Mutual respect, appropriate forms of leadership, management of conflict, active listening, and nonjudgmental responding are all essential ingredients of effective professional collaboration, as well as developmental supervision. In the consulting model, while the consultant is not a supervisor, they are in the position of an expert. In the coaching model, collaborators take turns coaching each other; they alternate taking a leadership role. In the teaming model, collaborators take the role of the team leader as the situation dictates. Collaboration does not mean that all participants are equal at all times. There is a need for collaborators to understand the principles of developmental supervision and situational leadership so that regardless of the role played in a collaborative relationship, each role is respected and valued. The overriding goal of either developmental supervision or of educational collaboration is institutional improvement and increased teaching effectiveness.

As collaborative practice has increased, common barriers to collaboration have been outlined by Allen-Meares and Pugach (1982). They suggest that the shift from isolated to collaborative teaching may be difficult. Impediments may be grouped according to the following categories:

- Philosophical differences
- Educational preparation
- Organizational/institutional practices
- Small-group dynamics

They recommend personnel preparation, district in-service, and research as three ways to address the barriers. The need for pre-service or in-service training has been echoed by Ayres and Meyer (1992) who propose that teachers and administrators should not be considered as passive consumers of training packages, but should be empowered to take ownership. A task force approach would allow the trainees to develop plans as a group effort and would reinforce collaborative practice.

The Keystone Project as described by Leggett and Hoyle (1987) incorporates an ongoing training for collegiality into the school culture. Teachers in Fort Worth, Texas, applied for admission to a four-week summer lab school. They were trained as cadre trainers who conducted staff development sessions at the district or school level, or as demonstration teachers who modeled lab school techniques in their classrooms while being observed by other teachers. Critical to this project was group-guided practice followed by peer coaching. Peer coaches collected data during observations and provided nonevaluative feedback. Through the project, teachers learned new teaching techniques, modeled them, and participated in peer coaching teams. The results were increased dialogue about instruction, sharing of instructional strategies, and quick assimilation of new teachers. Through collaborative training sessions, and using the clinical observation process for peer coaching, teachers were able to break the bonds of isolation and begin professional sharing.

Time is a pervasive problem in educational collaboration, whether for student growth, for staff development, or for problem solving. In a fast-paced society and complex modern culture, no one has time. Although teaming is required by special education mandate, and a group effort is required by civil rights legislation, the structure of the school has not changed. If teachers are lucky, they have a preparation period each day. Rarely, however, are prep periods scheduled so that teachers who want to collaborate are free at the same time. Teachers exchange information in the hall, during recess duty, or over a half-hour lunch period that has shrunk to twenty minutes after dismissing the students. Before-school meetings are impossible for some teachers, while after school is problematic for others. Time is often named as the biggest barrier to educational collaboration.

Raywid (1993) has described examples of creative ways to make time for professional collaboration. The examples can be categorized according to student grouping, personnel assignment, and calendar/scheduling changes.

In the category of student grouping, she suggests dividing students into "houses." While one "house" does community service, their teachers meet together. Community service can reflect curricular areas so that teachers from the same academic discipline have an opportunity to meet. Another strategy is administratively assigning students to schools within schools. Specialists (e.g., art, music, PE, etc.) rotate a program through the schools freeing content instructional teams for a half day of collaboration.

The second category of strategies for increasing collaborative time lies in the area of personnel assignment. Class size can be increased to allow for a surplus of teachers who become substitutes. Another strategy is staffing six teachers to four classes. This frees teachers on a rotating basis for collaboration purposes.

Calendar or scheduling changes are yet another category of ways to make time for collaboration. Collaborating teachers can be scheduled for the same lunch period with a common preparation period, either before or after lunch. Specials can be blocked so that teachers have a longer time for collaborative sessions. Lengthening the school day for four days and dismissing students at noon on the fifth will free an afternoon for cooperative planning sessions. Adding a required hour each day for teachers, either before or after student-required attendance will preclude the problem of before- or after-school conflicts to teacher collaboration sessions. Staff development days can be scheduled to allow for less time on a more frequent basis. Because most schools have more instructional days than are mandated by state laws, some instructional time can be converted into staff development time. One day per week can be designated "hobby day" with instruction in special interest areas by volunteers. Finally, adopting a year-round calendar with three-week intersessions permits concentrated meeting days for teacher teaming.

These three categories of suggestions by Raywid (1993) are all examples of structural changes proposed by Glatthorn (1987) as a necessary condition for cooperative professional development. Glatthorn suggests changes in the use of physical space to facilitate cooperation, changes in the school schedule to make working together possible, and assigning staff to foster cooperation.

As society has changed, so must education. Collaboration is not only necessary, it is required for students with special needs. Although collaboration has evolved from resource assistance to peer coaching and shared decision making, all three continue to be valid forms of cooperation among professionals. The model of collaboration used—consulting, coaching, or teaming—depends upon situation and purpose. Employing the process of clinical observation will provide for goal setting, collection of observational data, and objective data analysis for provision of technical assistance, collegial support, or challenge solutions. An understanding of appropriate collaborative leadership, providing for ongoing staff development, and allowing time for collaborative practice will offset barriers to collaboration. Educational programming for an increasingly diverse student population demands effective collaboration among educators and human services professionals. Their collaborative efforts will be more effective if they are accomplished within a framework for understanding and in a self-reflective manner.

OVERVIEW OF SUBSEQUENT CHAPTERS

This text will define three basic models of collaboration—consulting, coaching, and teaming. Three purposes for collaboration in education and the human services are technical improvement to meet student needs, collegial support for professional development, and group decision making for finding solutions to immediate or long-term challenges. With a legal foundation, and using clinical observation as a tool, each model will be discussed in terms of supports, barriers, and appropriate use. The impact of adult development and the need for situational leadership or developmental supervision add interest to any collaborative effort. Collaborative practice means change for most educators. Change involves conflict so the process of change, as well as key elements for successful change, are presented. To prevent unnecessary conflict, several decision-making models are presented. Finally, a systems approach to collaboration among educators and human service professionals is proposed. A general introduction having been provided in this first chapter, subsequent chapters present the following information:

- Chapter 2 details provisions of P.L. 94-142, IDEA, and Section 504 with regard to educational practice. Case law, the judiciary interpretation of legislation, reinforces the legal basis for collaborative practice.
- Chapter 3 presents the early work of Cogan (1973) in clinical supervision. This form of supervision was developed in order to provide a nonthreatening environment for growth rather than to evaluate current performance. Through data collection and analysis, clinical supervisory practice, renamed clinical observation, serves as a tool for professional collaboration, whether the collaborative purpose be technical assistance, collegial support, or challenge solution.
- Chapter 4 defines the traditional consulting model of special–general educational collaboration. The key to this model is assistance of an expert or master teacher to someone in need of guidance. Different examples of the model are described. The special educator as expert has been de-emphasized in order to recognize that general educators have their own areas of expertise and can also serve as consultants. The chapter lists supports for, barriers to, and appropriate use of consulting.
- Chapter 5 defines the coaching model of collaboration. In coaching, two or more professionals work to assist each other. The key to this model is parity as participants alternately coach or are coached. This chapter describes supports for, barriers to, and appropriate use of coaching.
- Chapter 6 defines the teaming model of collaboration. A teaming model is interactive so the key to this model is role release. Different members of the team provide expertise and/or leadership at different times depending upon situational needs. In a teaming model of collaboration, members of the team share ownership of the team's goals and results. The model is discussed in terms of supports, barriers, and appropriate use.
- Chapter 7 explores different purposes for collaboration. Three basic reasons for collaborating are technical assistance, collegial support, and challenge solution. Garmston (1987) has described these three purposes in reference to coaching, but each purpose applies equally to the consulting and teaming collaborative models.

- Chapter 8 increases awareness of the complexity of educational collaboratives by introducing the impact of adult developmental levels and career stages on collaboration. This chapter further complicates collaborative issues by exploring application of appropriate leadership and supervisory styles to collaborative efforts.
- Chapter 9 considers the process of changing behavior and the stages people go through in order to make major changes. Professional collaborative practice is a change for many teachers, but collaboration itself can ease the change process. The importance of flexibility and ability to problem solve are stressed. Several different decision-making processes that may be especially helpful in preventing conflict situations are presented.
- Chapter 10 presents the context for collaborative practice and proposes a systems approach to the implementation of models of collaboration throughout education and the human services.

COLLABORATION PORTFOLIO DEVELOPMENT THROUGH CHAPTER ACTIVITIES

Three activities are suggested at the end of each chapter in this text. Activities promote student development as collaborators and are to be included in a portfolio on collaboration. The first activity is personal application of the chapter topic to the student's current professional role. The second is a reflection on some aspect of the chapter. Students may be directed to one of the chapter references, asked to respond to the chapter vignette, or requested to respond personally to an issue discussed in the chapter. The third activity is an invitation to engage in action research. A research topic is proposed and students are asked to carry out a mini research project. This sequence corresponds to the three general purposes for collaboration—technical improvement, professional development, and challenge solution.

If an activity does not seem immediately applicable to the student's current role, personal ingenuity should be employed to modify, adapt, or otherwise mutate the activity as written. For educators, the adaptation of an activity may be as valuable as the activity itself. To meet the diverse needs of students, teachers and support personnel must continually adapt and modify standard curricula. The action research activities may not be readily accomplished within the framework of a semester course. These activities can be initiated by students with the understanding that they will be ongoing even past the end of an academic term. Alternately, plans for the suggested action research may be outlined with the intention of carrying out the project once the student returns to their workplace. Attempting to accomplish all three of each chapter's activities is not advised. Students may choose one or several of the activities to include in their individual portfolios.

The Purpose of Student Portfolio Development

Collaboration is itself a change process. Through personal application, professional reflection, and action research, collaborators can clarify problems to be addressed, reflect on causes and possible solutions, and evaluate their collaborative efforts by collecting and analyzing data. A portfolio of collaborative practice will document individual growth while promoting reflection on personal professional change.

Portfolios come in many guises and can be directed toward a variety of purposes (Truscott, et al., 1994). Cook and Kessler (1993) describe a portfolio for use in an employment interview. This type, similar to that of an artist or a journalist, contains evidence of professional competence to be shared with a potential employer. Such a portfolio is for display. Wolf (1991) promotes the teaching portfolio as a means of teacher evaluation. He maintains that a portfolio can be a means for mentoring, for supporting collegial interaction, and for promoting reflection on teaching. This type of product is a portfolio for workspace. The portfolio to be developed through the chapter activities is of the latter type, a portfolio for workspace directed toward growth as an educational collaborator.

The value of the portfolio in teacher education is increasingly recognized. Barton and Collins (1993) describe the application of portfolios for pre-service teacher training in the areas of literacy and science. They provide a rationale for portfolio use by contrasting the portfolio with a comprehensive exam. As opposed to written essay responses that are graded on a pass/fail basis, the portfolio provides insight into pre-service teacher development in the following ways:

- Taking into account the experiences encountered and professional duties performed
- Providing the opportunity for both students and faculty to reflect on student growth over time
- Shifting the ownership of learning onto the student
- Helping students to become more articulate
- Yielding insights for both students and faculty into individual performance throughout the course of their studies
- Promoting cognitive links to bridge theory and practice

In short, they describe this approach as allowing ". . . teachers to display their growing strengths, rather than simply exposing their weaknesses" (p. 209). The portfolio to be developed through each set of chapter activities will allow students to display their growing understanding and professional application of collaborative practice.

The promise of the portfolio has been discussed similarly by other teacher educators. Ohlhausen and Ford (1990) found that portfolios personalized assessment, encouraged reflective thinking, provided long-term perspective, and enhanced student accountability. Christensen and Walker (1992) found that undergraduate students frequently sought structure, clear-cut directions, and precise information from their professors in methods classes. The instructors proposed using portfolios and more self-reflection in college courses in order to promote student ownership and responsibility for learning. Stahle and Mitchell (1993) discovered that by using portfolios in courses, students began to feel that the course and classroom were "theirs" and that assignments had credibility. They suggested that by using the four steps of effective teacher training—theory, observation, practice and coaching (Joyce and Weil, 1986)—the chances that portfolio use would be transferred from methods classes to post college performance would be enhanced.

The collaboration portfolio will promote reflection about collaborative practice and enhance accountability with regard to that practice. Suggested activities support the student with a scaffold for their developing understanding and implementation of collaboration. Through the text, students will be introduced to the theory of collaboration; through the chapter activities, they will be coached through observation and practice of that theory. Consequently, in-school application of thoughtful collaborative practice should be enhanced.

The Value of Action Research

Glatthorn (1987) discusses action research as one of several avenues for professional collaboration. According to Glatthorn, collaborative research involves identifying a problem, deciding the specific research question and methodology, carrying out the research, and using the results. Conditions listed as supporting cooperative professional development in the form of research are similar to conditions supportive of any educational collaboration:

- Strong administrative leadership
- Climate of openness and trust
- Separation of evaluation from collaboration

- Distinct focus and shared language
- Provision of needed resources
- Structural changes such as use of physical space, scheduling adjustments, and staff assignments

Calhoun (1993) lists the benefits of action research as achievement of equity for students, improvement of the organization, promotion of site-based decision making, and development of collegial relations. She has expanded the concept of action research into three approaches with five considerations. Whether the action research is individual teacher research, collaborative research, or school-wide research, the following should be considered:

- Purpose and process
- Outside support
- Qualitative or quantitative data
- Audience
- Side effects

Before beginning any research, the question to be answered by the research effort should be posed along with a process for answering it. What is it that the researcher wants to know and how can they go about finding the information? Posing a research question defines the purpose for a research project and determining a means of answering that question outlines the research process. A teacher may want to know if an outside consultant or the school's teacher assistance team will be more effective in solving the challenge of students who pose severe maladaptive behaviors in class. The teacher may call for consultant services for one student and work with the teacher assistance team for another, then compare the outcomes in terms of acceptable school behavior on the parts of both students.

Outside support refers to the help needed for carrying out the research. In order to contract with a consultant, the teacher is going to need budgetary approval from the district administration. To work with the teacher assistance team, the teacher will require scheduling flexibility on the part of the building administration. Parental permission for employing the services of either an outside consultant or an in-school team with any individual may be necessary. Outside support is analogous to scaffolding a building under construction. It provides the framework for making action research possible. If necessary supports are not in place, the research project is doomed before it is begun.

The decision of whether to collect qualitative or quantitative data must be based on the research question to be answered. Qualitative data refers to such information as testimonials, interviews, log descriptions, and collection of artifacts. What type of behavior is viewed as problematic is an example of qualitative data. Quantitative data refers to quantifying the information. Tallies of how many, how frequent, or how long with reference to the problem behavior are examples of quantitative data. For answering many research questions, a combination of both types of data is appropriate.

Audience refers to anyone who may be interested in the answer to the action research question. In this example, although the teacher is interested in terms of improved student behavior, the district may be interested in the research for budgetary reasons. Allowing a building team to solve the problem is undoubtedly less expensive than contracting with an outside consultant. The building administrator may want to know how much time is involved in consulting versus team collaboration. More flexible scheduling will be needed for allowing a team meeting than for permitting a consultant–teacher conference. Parents will be an interested audience in terms of securing the best possible services for their children.

Side effects refer to indirect effects of the research. Side effects can be positive or negative. In the case of research comparing consultant to teacher assistance team effectiveness in addressing problematic behavior, a ripple effect could permeate throughout the classroom. The teacher might use strategies suggested by the consultant or those worked out through the teacher assistance team with other children whose inappropriate behaviors are less severe. The opposite effect might be escalation of unacceptable behavior as other students seek the attention being lavished on the center of the action research project. Consideration of possible side effects of research may facilitate a decision with regard to process.

Combining recommendations from both Glatthorn (1987) and Calhoun (1993) results in awareness that in-school research efforts by teachers promote collaboration under specific conditions. First teachers should clearly specify the type and purpose of their proposed research effort. They need support from the school administration and possibly from outside sources. Teacher researchers require interpersonal trust, time for collaboration, and space for their research. Teacher research should result in increased collaborative practice within the school and increased accountability to the community audience. Pursuing action research projects for inclusion in a collaboration portfolio will facilitate increased analysis of collaborative practice by novice collaborators. As a result of their research activities, students will better understand collaboration in practice and will be able to evaluate their own professional collaboration efforts.

Chapter activities should be collected into a portfolio format for the following reasons:

- To promote personal application of theoretical constructs
- To foster the habit of reflection on professional practice
- To introduce the feasibility and value of ongoing action research

Students are well advised to pursue only as many chapter activities as they have the time to fully develop. The value of the portfolio lies in the thoroughness of activity completion, rather than in the number of activities attempted. A professional portfolio should demonstrate qualitative, reflective growth, rather than quantity of superficial activity.

SUMMARY

This chapter has provided a rationale for a text on professional collaboration. As society has become more complex and educators must work with each other and with other human services providers in order to develop the most appropriate education for today's youth, an understanding of different collaborative models and the knowledge of their appropriate application are essential. The chapter has presented a brief history of the evolution of collaborative practice in education and the human services. Beginning as consulting in an indirect service delivery model, educational collaboration has evolved into peer coaching and interactive teaming. An overview of the text is provided with a preview of each succeeding chapter's contents. Finally, a rationale for developing a professional portfolio on collaborative growth through the activities in each chapter has been provided.

VIGNETTE REPRISE

Sarah was overwhelmed by the articles that she had read and the books to which she had been exposed about educational collaboration. She wondered how she would ever organize all of the new information she had gained. Her head was swimming. Even more perplexing was how she could apply what she had learned about collaborative practice when she returned to Blue Spruce following her graduate studies. Sarah needed a framework for thinking about collaboration, a structure on which to attach other variables and information impacting collaboration, and supports for her own application of collaboration in education.

PORTFOLIO ACTIVITIES

1. *Personal Application:* Begin your professional collaboration portfolio. What it will look like physically (e.g., three-ring binder, accordion folder, file box, etc.). Into what sections will you want to separate it and how will you divide the sections? Where will you store it? What materials will you need?

2. *Professional Reflection:* Think about your professional role. Have you been involved in action research as an individual, with others, or at the school level? Describe the research and your involvement in terms of the five areas presented by Calhoun (1993): purpose and process, outside support, data, audience, and side effects.

3. *Action Research:* Choose one of the examples of gaining time for collaboration (Raywid, 1993). Develop an hypothesis regarding its potential effect on your current collaborative efforts. What outside supports do you need? Try it out and collect data regarding your implementation. What audience might be interested in your project? What are the side effects?

REFERENCES

Allen-Meares, P., and Pugach, M. (1982). "Facilitating Interdisciplinary Collaboration on Behalf of Handicapped Children and Youth." *Teacher Education and Special Education* 5(1): 30–36.

Ayres, B., and Meyer, L. (February 1992). "Helping Teachers Manage the Inclusive Classroom." *School Administrator:* 30–37.

Barton, J., and Collins, A. (1993). "Portfolios in Teacher Education." *Journal of Teacher Education* 44(3): 200–210.

Calhoun, E.F. (1993). "Action Research: Three Approaches." *Educational Leadership* 51(2): 62–65.

Christensen, L., and Walker, B.J. (1992). "Researching One's Own Teaching in a Reading Education Course." In N. Padak, T. Rasinski, and J. Logan (eds.), *Literacy Research and Practice: Foundations for the Year 2000,* 57–63. Pittsburgh, KS: College Reading Association.

Cogan, M.L. (1973). *Clinical Supervision.* Boston: Houghton Mifflin Co.

Cook, D., and Kessler, J. (1993). "The Professional Teaching Portfolio: A Useful Tool for an Effective Job Search." *ASCUS Annual* 15.

Cook L., and Friend, M. (1991). "Collaboration in Special Education: Coming of Age in the 1990s." *Preventing School Failure* 35(2): 24–27.

Garmston, R.J. (1987). "How Administrators Support Peer Coaching." *Educational Leadership* 44(5): 18–26.

Glatthorn, R.J. (1987). "Cooperative Professional Development: Peer-Centered Options for Teacher Growth." *Educational Leadership* 45(3): 31–35.

Glickman, C.D. (1990). *Supervision of Instruction: A Developmental Approach,* 2d ed. Boston: Allyn and Bacon.

Glickman, C.D., Gordon, S.P., and Ross-Gordon, J.M. (1995). *Supervision of Instruction: A Developmental Approach,* 3d ed. Boston: Allyn and Bacon.

Hanson, M.J., and Widerstrom, A.H. (1992). "Consultation and Collaboration: Essentials of Integration Efforts for Young Children." In C.A. Peck, S.L. Odom, and D.D. Bricker (eds.), *Integrating Young Children with Disabilities into Community Programs: Ecological Perspectives on Research and Implementation,* 149–168. Baltimore: Paul H. Brookes Publishing Co.

Heron, T.E., and Harris, K.C. (1993). *The Educational Consultant.* Austin, TX: Pro-Ed.

Idol, L. (1993). *Special Educator's Consultation Handbook.* Austin, TX: Pro-Ed.

Idol, L., Nevin, A., and Paolucci-Whitcomb, P. (1994). *Collaborative Consultation.* Austin, TX: Pro-Ed.

Idol, L., Paolucci-Whitcomb, P., and Nevin, A. (1987) *Collaborative Consultation.* Austin, TX: Pro-Ed.

Idol, L., and West, J.F. (1991). "Educational Collaboration: A Catalyst for Effective Schooling." *Intervention in School and Clinic* 27(2): 70–78, 125.

Johnson, L.J., Pugach, M.C., and Devlin, S. (1990). "Professional Collaboration: Challenges of the Next Decade." *Teaching Exceptional Children* 22(2): 9–11.

Joyce, B., and Weil, M. (1986). *Models of Teaching,* 3d ed. Englewood Cliffs, NJ: Prentice-Hall, Inc.

Leggett, D., and Hoyle, S. (1987). "Preparing Teachers for Collaboration." *Educational Leadership* 45(3): 58–63.

Mandeville, G.K., and Rivers, J. (1989). "Is the Hunter Model a Recipe for Supervision?" *Educational Leadership* 46(8): 39–43.

McFaul, S.A., and Cooper, J.M. (1984). "Peer Clinical Supervision: Theory vs. Reality." *Educational Leadership* 41(7): 4–9.

Morsink, C.V., Thomas, C.C., and Correa, V.I. (1991). *Interactive Teaming: Consultation and Collaboration in Special Programs.* New York: Merrill-Macmillan Publishing Co.

Ohlhausen, M.M., and Ford, M.P. (1990). "Portfolio Assessment in Teacher Education: A Tale of Two Cities." Paper presented at the annual meeting of the National Reading Conference, Miami. ERIC Document Reproduction Service No. ED 329 917.

Pugach, M.C., and Johnson, L.J. (1995). *Collaborative Practitioners Collaborative Schools.* Denver: Love Publishing Co.

Raywid, M.A. (1993). "Finding Time for Collaboration." *Educational Leadership* 51(1): 30–34.

Stahle, D.L., and Mitchell, J.P. (1993). "Portfolio Assessment in College Methods Courses: Practicing What We Preach." *Journal of Reading* 36(7): 538–542.

Sugai, G.M., and Tindal, G.A. (1993). *Effective School Consultation.* Pacific Grove, CA: Brooks/Cole Publishing Co.

Truscott, D.M., Christensen, L., Walker, B.J., Robichaud, B.A., Ayres, B., Fishbaugh, M.S., and Gregory, S.P. (1994). "Scaffolding Reflectivity through Portfolios." *Journal of Reading Education* 20(1): 33–42.

Voltz, D.L. (1993). "Collaboration: Just What Do You Mean, 'Collaborate'?" *L.D. Forum* 17(4): 32–34.

Welch, M., and Sheridan, S.M. (1995). *Educational Partnerships Serving Students at Risk.* Fort Worth, TX: Harcourt Brace College Publishers.

West, J.F., Idol, L., and Cannon, G. (1989). *Collaboration in the Schools.* Austin, TX: Pro-Ed.

Wiederholt, J.L., Hammill, D.D., and Brown, V.L. (1983). *The Resource Teacher: A Guide to Effective Practices.* Austin, TX: Pro-Ed.

Wolf, K. (1991). "The School Teacher's Portfolio: Issues in Design, Implementation, and Evaluation." *Phi Delta Kappan* 73(2): 129–136.

2

LEGAL FOUNDATIONS FOR COLLABORATION

Vignette

One crisp fall morning, when the high line's big sky was a clear blue, and the prairie grasses were dry and brown, Joe was enrolled in Blue Spruce School's program for young children with disabilities. Joe was a four-year-old boy with fetal alcohol effects and autistic-like behaviors. He was a tiny child for his age, with big, wide-set eyes, and a rather flat nose that ran constantly. Joe could not walk unassisted when he was enrolled in the preschool. At home, he either crawled on the floor, or was confined to his stroller. Joe had few self-help skills. He was still in diapers and could not feed himself. During his first morning in school, he rolled around the floor, sucked anything that happened to land in his little fist, and screamed. The special education teacher, Sarah, came to know Joe quite well. She spent many hours walking Joe through the halls, feeding him lunch, and making regular trips to the boys' restroom. Gradually, Sarah faded her own involvement with Joe, and increased the preschool and kindergarten teachers' responsibility for him. With the assistance of the kindergarten classroom assistant, Joe was weaned from diapers, and learned to feed himself. He continued to scream, however, especially when demands were made of him. Because he had no intelligible expressive language, the teachers, speech therapist, and assistant who were working with Joe attended a summer institute on assistive technology. As a first step toward Joe's using a computer for communication, Sarah developed a board with pictures of his most common communication needs. With the use of the "quick board" pictures, Joe began to communicate in a limited way and gain some control over his environment. When Sarah left for her graduate studies, Joe was fully included in a general education first grade classroom. He had begun meeting first grade behavioral expectations since being given his own

*desk. He was communicating using a computer, as well as his quick board of
pictures. In fact, the first grade teacher, who had dreaded Joe's presence in her
classroom since he was in preschool, called a team meeting and suggested that
Sarah's substitute, her special education assistant, and the speech therapist
decrease the amount of time spent in the first grade classroom. Joe was remain-
ing on task longer, acting in more socially acceptable ways, and interacting
more positively with the other children when not being smothered by their well-
intentioned assistance. The insight and opinions of all team members were considered essential before any change in Joe's educational program could be made.*

Chapter Outline

Vignette

Chapter Outline

Chapter Content

Summary

Vignette Reprise

Portfolio Activities

References

FEDERAL LAW

IDEA

In 1975, Congress passed P.L. 94-142, The Education for All Handicapped Children Act. The law resulted from parental advocacy for their
children. This landmark legislation demonstrated Congress's intent to

right injustice previously imposed on persons with disabilities by the schools (Martin, 1990). Before 1975, schools discriminated against students in at least the following ten ways:

- One million students were excluded from public schools.
- If in school, the unique needs of special education students were not met.
- If in school, special education students were often excluded from appropriate programs through expulsion or suspension.
- Evaluations, often culturally or linguistically biased, did not address individual needs.
- Special education had no goals and no way to assess educational progress.
- Children with disabilities were segregated from their nondisabled peers.
- Reasons were given by schools for excluding students.
- Parents were not involved in educational decisions made about their children.
- Parents were denied access to their children's educational records.
- Parents had no impartial grievance procedure to pursue if they disagreed with their children's program.

With P.L. 94-142, and its subsequent revisions, Congress mandated the ways in which schools were to redress these grievances.

The 1990 revision of special education law is P.L. 101-476, the Individuals with Disabilities Education Act (IDEA). This law defines thirteen categories of disabilities that qualify a student for special education services: deaf; deaf-blind; hearing impaired (HI); mentally retarded (MR); multiple disabilities; orthopedically impaired (OI); other health impaired (OHI); seriously emotionally disabled (ED); specific learning disability (LD); speech impaired; visually impaired (VI); autism; and traumatic brain injury (TBI). IDEA addresses previous injustices in the following ways:

- A free and appropriate public education (FAPE) must be provided for students with disabilities.
- The unique needs of students with disabilities are recognized through the thirteen disability categories defined by law.
- Students must be provided access to programs educationally appropriate for them, and may not be arbitrarily excluded.
- Evaluations must be nonbiased and conducted by a multidisciplinary team.
- For each student with a disability, an individualized educational program (IEP) must be developed with long-term goals and short-term objectives.

- Students must be educated with their nondisabled peers in the least restrictive environment (LRE) possible.
- Related services must be provided for the student by the school if those services are necessary for the student's gaining benefit from his or her education.
- Program planning for the student must be accomplished by a team including the student's parents, as well as teachers and other school personnel.
- Compliance with the Federal Educational Right to Privacy Act (FERPA) insures that special education records remain confidential, but that parents and the student with disabilities have a right to access those records.
- Means are provided for parents or school officials to object to an individual's educational program through a formal due process procedure.

IDEA, as enabling legislation, is a source of funding for special education services. Through this law, Congress appropriates federal tax dollars through state educational agencies (SEA) to local districts. In order to access their allocations, states and local educational agencies (LEA) must develop a plan and submit it to the Office of Special Education Programs (OSEP), a division of the Office of Special Education and Rehabilitation Services (OSERS). The plan must include several components. There must be provision for the following:

- Identification of children in need of special education (childfind)
- Computation of costs over and above the average cost per general education student (federal special education allocations must supplement, not supplant, general education dollars)
- Delineation of procedural safeguards (FERPA, evaluation and IEP processes, due process procedures, etc.)
- Development of a comprehensive system of personnel development (CSPD) council to conduct regular needs assessments, provide ongoing technical assistance and in-service training, and disseminate information
- Support for a state special education advisory panel

Compliance with this sweeping legislation necessitates collaboration. There has to be teamwork between state and local level educators and among personnel on both levels. Parents of special needs children and educational assistants who work with students with disabilities are included as team members. Related services professionals, such as speech therapists, occupational therapists, physical therapists, psychologists, community agency personnel, and others may be essential team participants. Without collaboration among all stakeholders, the varied components of IDEA cannot be properly implemented.

The 1986 revision of P.L. 94-142 extended the special education mandate beyond what is generally accepted as school age. P.L. 99-457 provided for early intervention with infants, toddlers, and preschoolers with disabilities and mandated transition program planning for sixteen-year-old students who receive special educational services for more than fifty percent of their school day. The individual family service plan (IFSP) for young children addresses more than educational needs. This plan provides for wrap-around services that take into consideration the child's entire environment. In order to develop a school-to-work transition plan for adolescents with disabilities, human service agencies other than the high school must be involved. The provisions of P.L. 99-457, which are reinforced through IDEA, cannot be implemented by individuals in isolation; they demand collaboration.

The collaboration necessary to effectively implement IDEA may be in the form of consulting, coaching, or teaming. The consulting model readily applies to the individual family service plan. Programs for very young children usually involve home visits by the special education teacher. The program is brought to the home, rather than bringing the child to school. The teacher serves as a consultant to the parents as they learn to work with their child in developmentally appropriate ways. During the school years, from kindergarten through twelfth grade, the coaching model is often employed as teachers assist one another in dealing with difficult students or in attempting new models of teaching. As students transition from school to work, the teaming model is apparent. Special and general education personnel meet with vocational rehabilitation and employment counselors to develop an individual transition plan (ITP). These examples are oversimplified; actual applications of any of the three models throughout a child's eligibility for IDEA services, from birth to twenty-one, are innumerable.

Section 504

Section 504 of the Rehabilitation Act of 1973 is not special education legislation. It does not enable programming by allocation of funds. Section 504 is a civil rights law that prohibits discrimination on the basis of disability. Educational institutions discriminate against students with disabilities when they fail to provide equal access to programs and facilities, so that students can enjoy benefit from their education equal to that enjoyed by their nondisabled peers. Subpart D of

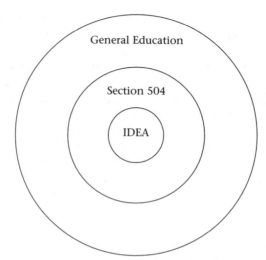

FIGURE 2.1   Section 504 Eligible Students

this act pertains to preschool, elementary, and secondary education. Section 504 demands that general educators modify curricula and facilities in order to accommodate the special needs of students with disabilities, whether or not students qualify for special education services under IDEA.

Students qualify for Section 504 accommodations if they have or are perceived to have a physical or mental disability that severely interferes with a major life activity. All IDEA students qualify for Section 504 consideration, but not all Section 504 students qualify for special education. Figure 2.1 shows the relationships among general education students, students who qualify for Section 504 considerations, and students who are eligible for special education under IDEA. The large circle refers to all students in our public educational system. A subpart of this population of students are students who need accommodations under Section 504 in order to access education. The inner circle holds those students who receive special education services. In addition to special education, these students require considerations of accessibility under Section 504, and they are a subpart of the total school population.

Students with a chronic illness such as asthma or diabetes, or an acute condition such as pregnancy or AIDS, may receive Section 504 services. Students with a history of substance abuse may not be discriminated against if they have been through a treatment program and are not current users. General educators must make accommodation for students with ADD/ADHD in order for them to have a better chance for academic success. School personnel must determine the risk posed to other students by an individual with a contagious disease or severe behavior problems, and what constitutes a "reasonable accommodation" for the individual.

Section 504 complements IDEA's special educational mandates with procedural requirements that parallel IDEA (Figure 2.2). Schools must provide the following:

- A free and appropriate public education (FAPE)
- SEA/LEA interpretation of Section 504's vague definition of disability
- Equal access to educational programs
- An informal, although multidimensional assessment of the student's educational strengths and needs
- A general education intervention plan (GEIP) for the student
- Accommodations in the general educational environment
- Provision of specialized educational services as necessary
- Notification to parents that their child is receiving a modified educational program
- Confidentiality of records, and parental access according to FERPA regulations
- A grievance procedure to be followed for addressing charges of discrimination

IDEA	Section 504
<ul><li>Guarantees Free & Appropriate Public Education</li><li>Defines thirteen Categories of Disabilities</li><li>Guarantees Access to Appropriate Programs</li><li>Mandates a Multidisciplinary Assessment</li><li>Mandates an Individualized Education Program</li><li>Mandates Placement in the Least Restrictive Environment</li><li>Provides Related Services</li><li>Requires Parental Participation and Permission</li><li>Complies with the Federal Educational Right to Privacy Act</li><li>Provides a Due Process Procedure for Disputes</li></ul>	<ul><li>Guarantees FAPE</li><li>Defines Disability as an Impairment Limiting a Major Life Activity</li><li>Guarantees Equal Access to Facilities/Programs</li><li>Requires Assessment by a Group Knowledgeable about the Student and the Suspected Disability</li><li>Requires a General Education Intervention Plan</li><li>Requires Modifications and Adaptations in the General Education Classroom</li><li>Provides Specialized Educational Services</li><li>Requires Notification of Parents</li><li>Complies with FERPA</li><li>Provides for a Grievance Procedure</li></ul>

FIGURE 2.2   IDEA/Section 504 Comparison Chart

Although no funds are appropriated to help schools implement this law, federal funds can be withheld from entire districts if the Office of Civil Rights (OCR) which administrates Section 504 finds noncompliance on the part of individual schools. Similar to IDEA, Section 504 cannot be properly implemented without a team effort; collaboration among education and human services professionals is essential.

The three models of collaboration apply to compliance with Section 504, just as easily as to compliance with IDEA. For students who are at-risk of school failure but who do not qualify for special education services, the consulting model is often employed. Special education teachers with expertise in working with learning disabilities or cognitive delays can assist general educators as they struggle with the academic achievement of at-risk students. Special educators use the coaching model to help as general educators expand their repertoire of teaching techniques. Use of the teaming model is necessary when several teachers, classroom assistants, and school administrators must consistently carry out a behavioral plan for students with severe behavioral disorders who do not qualify as students with emotional disabilities. Meeting the Section 504 requirements for general educational modifications and adaptations is not feasible without collaboration.

ADA and GOALS 2000

The Americans with Disabilities Act extends the nondiscrimination mandate of Section 504 from programs receiving federal funding to the private sector. According to a 1993 Senate Education Committee Report (LDA Newsbriefs, 1994), the ADA rests on the premise that disability is a natural part of the human experience. Individuals with disabilities have the right to live independently, make choices, contribute to society, and enjoy full inclusion and integration in all aspects of American society. The ADA definition of an individual with a disability differs from both the specificity of IDEA's categories and the generality of Section 504. According to the ADA, an individual with a disability is a person ". . . who, with or without reasonable modifications to rules, policies, or practices, the removal of architectural, communication, or transportation barriers, or the provision of auxiliary aids and services, meets the essential eligibility requirements for the receipt of services or the participation in programs or activities provided by a public entity" (42 U.S.C.A. §12131). Although the ADA primarily focuses on nondiscriminatory transportation and employment practices, its emphasis on accessibility to facilities and programs affects educational institutions. The ADA impacts all aspects of American life including education.

A recent educational initiative from Washington is GOALS 2000: Educate America Act. According to the Senate Education Committee Report, July 1993 (LDA Newsbriefs, 1994), the needs of students with disabilities have been considered throughout this legislation, so that America's educational goals are applicable to all students. The committee has addressed students with disabilities in each of the six national education goals:

- School readiness
- School completion
- Student achievement and citizenship
- Mathematics and science
- Adult literacy and lifelong learning
- Safe, disciplined, and drug-free schools

The intent of both Section 504 and the ADA has been applied to GOALS 2000, so that rather than discriminating against persons with disabilities, the education act's mandates can be appropriately adapted and modified. In requiring nondiscrimination throughout American society, and in applying this precept to schools, the ADA and GOALS 2000 promote collaborative practice. A more inclusive society and more inclusive schools demand teamwork.

Inclusive educational practice can be defined as acceptance of each individual student according to their abilities and disabilities into the mainstream of public education. Inclusion is not mandated by any of our current laws but is supported by the least restrictive environment clause of IDEA, by the accessibility standard of Section 504, and by case law from the federal court system. IDEA mandates a continuum of services from a general educational setting without supports through part-time resource assistance, full time special class placement, special day schools, and residential schools, to the most restrictive settings of hospital or home. The actual placement determined to be the least restrictive environment for a student's education is decided by the individual education program team, based on an individual student's needs and goals. Inclusive educational practice is a philosophy based on an educational imperative to change the school to fit the student, rather than to change the student to fit the school. Inclusive practice demands that students be educated with their peers, that educational expectations be determined on an individual student basis, that students be separated according to the continuum of services for temporary periods only, and that teachers have the support and assistance they need to educate all students. Inclusive educational practice means that students are "innocent until proven guilty." They must prove that they require extra help

Inclusion Is	Inclusion Is Not
• All students • Special assistance as needed • Natural proportions • Differing expectations for individuals • Appropriate class size • Collaborative approach • Resources and Supports • In-service training • Ongoing technical assistance	• Placement by category • Once in resource, always in resource • All special needs students in one class • Expecting all students to achieve similarly in the standard curriculum • Thirty students, one teacher, ability extremes • One teacher, alone, meeting student needs • Lack of necessary services, funds, and materials • Untrained teachers responsible for all • One-time training with no follow-up

FIGURE 2.3 Inclusive Educational Practice

in a segregated setting before being placed in that setting, as opposed to proving that they can succeed in the mainstream of education before being educated with their peers (see Figure 2.3).

CASE LAW

Case law results from judicial interpretation of legislation made as a result of legal disputes. Redress of grievances under IDEA begins with a local due process procedure. If both parties are not satisfied with the decision of a hearing officer, they may appeal to the state education agency. The state may name a mediator for the dispute. If the parties to the dispute are still not satisfied, they may appeal to federal district and appellate courts. The final appeal is made to the Supreme Court.

Not all disputes are accepted by the Supreme Court. Cases are chosen if they meet one of the following three criteria:

• Rendering a precise legal interpretation
• Resolution of conflict between lower court rulings
• Identification of a legal standard

The importance of a judicial decision rests on how broadly the standard and result can be generalized.

The Section 504 grievance procedure is quite different from IDEA's due process. If anyone suspects discrimination on the basis of disability, they can go directly to the Office of Civil Rights (OCR). The complainant then ceases to be a party in the case. OCR conducts an on-site investigation during which the single complaint may become a class action suit. Although confidentiality of individual identification must be maintained, school records pertinent to the complaint become part of the public domain.

IDEA case law has supported inclusive practice through a liberal interpretation of the least restrictive environment (LRE) clause. Issues addressed by the court include:

- Defining "appropriate" education
- Defining related services
- Stressing the central role of an individualized education program
- Emphasizing parental participation
- Limiting disciplinary policy
- Aligning state and local education agency responsibility for special programs (Martin, 1990)

The cases indirectly support collaboration because inclusion of students with disabilities in general education classes is not feasible without a team effort.

Defining "Appropriate" Education

One of the first P.L. 94-142 due process procedure cases to reach the Supreme Court was *Board of Education v. Rowley* (1982). Amy Rowley was a deaf child who was achieving well in school, but not commensurate with her ability. Her parents requested an interpreter in each class so that Amy could receive maximum benefit from her education. The school had provided an office teletype for phone contact with the parents, daily tutoring, speech therapy for three hours per week, and an FM hearing aid. The court decided that special education must be designed so that the unique needs of an individual are met and education is meaningful. In methodology, the school must go beyond standard procedures by choosing and disseminating promising practices. However, the court said that schools could look at the floor, not the ceiling, of educational services. The court found that Amy was receiving benefit from her educational opportunities in the mainstream without extensive accommodations. In considering the totality of a program, the court supported inclusive practice by stating that education can be defined by more than academic achievement.

For Amy to remain in the general education program there had to be collaboration among all parties. The school had been working with Amy's parents by providing special equipment for communicating with them. Amy's teacher and the speech pathologist had to collaborate in order for Amy to benefit from both her daily school work and her weekly speech and language therapy sessions. The school had to collaborate with consultants or with institutions of higher education in order to learn and apply new methods for working with Amy. Given the hearing loss that Amy experienced, she could not have achieved academically as well as she did without collaboration among everyone involved.

Defining Related Services

Related services were defined as services needed for the qualifying child with a disability to reach, enter, and remain in school by *Irving I.S.D. v. Tatro* (1984). The service need not be expensive or an undue burden. There are three qualifiers for a related service:

- The student has a disability according to IDEA.
- The service is needed in order for the child to benefit from education.
- The service need not be performed by a physician.

Amber Tatro had spina bifida and required catheterization. The school gave her parents three options—homebound instruction, catheterization in school by one of her parents, or placement in a class for students with severe disabilities. Amber's parents contended that catheterization was a related service as defined by law and the court agreed. This case supports inclusive practice by directing schools to provide needed related services for students so that they can remain in school with their peers.

The mandate that schools provide needed related services for students with disabilities demands collaboration across human service organizations. Related services can involve specialized therapy, such as that provided by speech and language pathologists, occupational therapists, or physical therapists. Related services can involve social workers, counselors, psychologists, or rehabilitation professionals. In Amber's case, the school teachers and administrators worked with medical personnel in order for Amber to remain in school. However, the possibilities for related services are endless. If the related service is to benefit the student educationally, then the professional educators and related service providers have to collaborate effectively.

Stressing the IEP and Emphasizing Parental Participation

The importance of developing an IEP according to proper procedure was emphasized in *Burlington School Committee v. Massachusetts Department of Education* (1985) (Martin, 1990). The facts of this case involve a child placed in a private school by his parents who objected to the public school's IEP. The decision in the case rested on provision of a "proper" IEP. "Proper" was defined as meaning that all provisions and correct procedures were in place. Especially important was parental involvement in IEP development.

This case directly supports collaboration by stressing the central role of parents in developing educational programs for students with disabilities. IDEA states that an IEP must be developed by a team of people and specifies necessary individuals for each of the thirteen categories of disability. Unless the IEP is written collaboratively by all vested parties, it is not valid. Noncompliance with special education procedural requirements constitutes a major violation of federal law and can result in severe repercussions for the school.

Limiting Disciplinary Policy

Limits were placed on school discipline policies in *Honig v. Doe* (1988). John Doe was a student with physical disabilities. He was teased to the point of an angry outburst by Jack Smith, a student with emotional disabilities who was prone to verbal impulsivity. A fight broke out when John attacked Jack. The school recommended expulsion with indefinite suspension pending a due process decision. The court determined that Congress's intent was to strip schools of the ability to expel students. Expulsion is a change of placement and requires a change in the IEP. Schools retain three options:

- In-school suspension
- Ten-day out-of-school placement
- Referral to the court to demonstrate exhaustion of administrative remedy and/or that the student is a danger to self or another

This case promotes inclusive educational practice by limiting the right of a school to arbitrarily exclude any student.

Limitations on arbitrary and capricious disciplinary actions against students mean that school personnel must collaborate to provide behavioral supports for students with emotional disabilities. Teachers, educational assistants, and school administrators may collaborate with a behavior consultant to develop expectations and consequences for student behavior. Once the plan is in place, they would work consistently across school employees and programs to carry it out. School faculty and staff might coach each other to ensure consistency in plan process and procedures. Only with consistent expectations do students with behavioral problems have a chance of achieving educationally appropriate and socially acceptable behavior. Only by collaborating as a team can the school personnel provide the necessary structure for these students.

Aligning State and Local Education Agency Responsibility

Delmuth v. Muth (1989) (Martin, 1990) clearly defined the state education agency as support for the local school. Parents who had requested private placement for their child with a disability were forced to follow a cumbersome state process. The court granted monetary remuneration to the parents on the basis of the inappropriate procedural requirements. As a result of this case, Congress revisited the state's sovereign immunity from being sued under the Eleventh Amendment. IDEA specifically states that a state education agency can be sued. The case supports collaboration between and among all levels of education as an essential component for compliance with special education law.

Considerations for Inclusion

Two cases decided in lower courts delineated a four-pronged test for determining if inclusion of a student with a disability in general education is the appropriate educational placement. Neill Roncker was an elementary-aged child with severe mental retardation and in need of special education services. Neill was placed in a special school. His parents requested that services be provided in a setting where he could have contact with nondisabled peers (*Roncker v. Walter,* 1983). Daniel R.R. was a student with significant mental retardation (*Daniel R.R. v. State Board of Education,* 1989). Similarly, Daniel's parents disagreed with his placement in a self-contained special education classroom. They wanted Daniel in a general education classroom. Neither case was won by the plaintiffs; in both cases, the courts decided in favor of a more restrictive setting. Nevertheless, the cases are important because of the following four deciding principles:

- Educational benefit for the student with disabilities
- Nonacademic benefit for the student with disabilities
- Effect of the student's presence on the other students
- Cost of inclusion either in personnel time or in money for providing the necessary supplementary aids and services

Using this four-pronged test, the courts have found in favor of including both Rachel Holland, a child with moderate mental retardation (*Board of Education of Sacramento Unified School District v. Holland,* 1992), and Raphael Oberti, a boy with Down's Syndrome and significant behavioral disabilities in general educational settings (*Oberti v. Clementon Board of Education,* 1993).

In the Roncker decision, the court stated that neither party to the complaint was satisfied with a proposed split attendance scheme. The court questioned how attendance in a special school with lunch, recess, and gym in a general education setting might be accomplished. The implication from the court was that appellant and appellee would have to collaborate in order for Neill Roncker's placement to be educationally beneficial.

The burden of proof for restrictive educational programming in settings removed from the educational mainstream lies with the school and is difficult to support. Case law, resulting from court responses to both IDEA and Section 504, has consistently reinforced inclusive practice. In so doing, the courts have promoted collaboration. Without teamwork, inclusion is not feasible.

PROFESSIONAL ASSOCIATION POLICY

Policy statements from professional education organizations seem polarized with regard to inclusive educational practice, but upon closer scrutiny may be perceived as mere arguments in semantics. The American Federation of Teachers (AFT) (Gorman and Rose, 1994) and the Learning Disabilities Association of America (LDA) have both made strong position statements against full inclusion. Their opposition, however, rests on implementation of inclusive practice without attention to class size, teacher education, and needed supports. Both groups state that expecting all students to achieve equally in the same manner is unrealistic and detrimental to all students' achievement. Groups such as the National Education Association (NEA) and the Council of Administrators of Special Education (CASE), both of which strongly support inclusion, would not disagree with specific objections as voiced by the AFT and LDA. Inclusive educational practice demands proper implementation; otherwise, what is being done in the name of inclusive educational practice is in reality "dumping." For students with a broad range of types and severity of disabilities to participate in general education requires the work of many hands and the thoughts of many minds. Without collaborative practice, opposition to inclusion is justified.

SUMMARY

This chapter has provided a legal foundation for collaboration among education and human services professionals. Both special education mandate, IDEA, and general education civil rights legislation, Section 504, cannot be implemented without collaboration. IDEA requires a multidisciplinary team for evaluation and program planning; Section 504 demands that a group knowledgeable about assessment, the student, and the School's resources convene to develop a general education intervention plan. Federal policy, as reflected in the Americans with Disabilities Act and in GOALS 2000, further supports the need for teamwork. Court decisions, from the Supreme Court and from lower federal jurisdictions reinforce the concept of collaboration among professionals and others with an interest in an individual child's educational program. Finally, policy statements with regard to inclusion of students with disabilities in general educational programs, whether the statement is pro or con inclusion, reinforce the need for professional educational collaboration.

VIGNETTE REPRISE

Joe's enrollment in Blue Spruce School was questioned by some, but supported by inclusion advocates. However, his legal right to be there was without question. Clearly the intent of both special education and general education legislation is a free and appropriate public education in the least restrictive environment. Although Joe required individual attention, major modification of the general education curriculum, and radically different expectations from the average student, the need to move him to a more restrictive placement would be difficult to prove in court. To continue including Joe in Blue Spruce School, however, meant increasing collaborative efforts on the parts of all those involved in his education.

PORTFOLIO ACTIVITIES

1. *Personal Application:* Obtain a copy of GOALS 2000. Apply the goals to your classroom by planning specific implementation strategies for each. Adapt your plan for one or more students with disabilities included in your classroom.

2. *Professional Reflection:* Read one or more of the court cases discussed in this chapter. Summarize the facts of the case and reflect on the potential impact of this case in your current professional role.

3. *Action Research:* Survey your school/district with regard to compliance to Section 504.

Ask the following questions:

- What is Section 504?
- Who is the Section 504 compliance coordinator?
- What is the Section 504 process?
- What kind of accommodations are made for students and how are they documented?
- What is the Section 504 grievance procedure?

Collect and analyze your data. Who might be the audience for your research? What might be the side effects of your research?

REFERENCES

Americans with Disabilities Act of 1990. 42 U.S.C.A. §§12101–12213 (West Supp., 1992).

Board of Education of Sacramento U.S.D. v. Holland, 786 F. Supp. 847 (E.D. Cal., 1992).

Board of Education v. Rowley, 458 U.S. 176, 102 S.Ct. 3034, 73 L.Ed. 2d 690 (1982).

Council of Administrators of Special Education. (1993). *CASE Future Agenda for Special Education: Creating a Unified Education System.* Reston, VA: Council for Exceptional Children.

Daniel R.R. v. State Board of Education, 874 F. 2d 1036 (5th Cir. 1989).

Education of All Handicapped Children Act of 1975. P.L. 94-142. U.S.C. §1401 (1975).

Gorman, T., and Rose, M. (March, 1994). "Inclusion: Taking a Stand." *American Teacher 78*(6): 9–12.

Honig v. Doe, 484 U.S. 108, S.Ct. 592, 98 L.Ed. 2d 686 (1988).

Individuals with Disabilities Education Act. P.L. 101-476. U.S.C. §§1401–1468 (1990).

Irving I.S.D. v. Tatro, 468 U.S. 883, 104 S.Ct. 3371, 82 L.Ed. 2d 664 (1984).

Learning Disabilities Association of America. (May/June, 1994). Inclusion. *LDA/Newsbriefs.*

Martin, R., J.D. (1990). "Tape 1: Overview of Public Law 94-142: The Wrongs Congress Required Schools to Right." In *Legal Challenges in Special Education.* Urbana, IL: Carle Media.

Martin, R., J.D. (1990). "Tape 2: The Supreme Court Cases on Public Law 94-142." In *Legal Challenges in Special Education.* Urbana, IL: Carle Media.

National Education Association. (1994). *NEA Today 13*(2): 16–17.

Oberti v. Clementon Board of Education, 995 F. 2d 1204 (3d Cir. 1993).

P.L. 99-457. 20 U.S.C. §1471 *et seq.* (1986).

Rehabilitation Act of 1973, Section 504. 29 U.S.C. 794 (1978).

Roncker v. Walter, 700 F. 2d 1058 (6th Cir. 1983), cert. den. 464 U.S. 864, 104 S.Ct. 196, 78 L.Ed. 2d 171 (1983).

3

CLINICAL OBSERVATION

Vignette

Sarah had participated in the teacher assistance team (TAT) in Blue Spruce School. Mandated by the state, this team was part of the special education prereferral process. When a teacher first attempted to refer a student for special education, the TAT went into action. The team's purpose was to recommend classroom accommodations and curricular adaptations which might change an individual student's behavioral or academic failure into success. Other team members included the High Line Special Education Cooperative school psychologist, the second grade teacher, and the ninth grade teacher. When a teacher needed assistance with a student, these four individuals talked with the teacher, observed the child in the classroom, took notes, and offered advice on programmatic changes. Usually little change resulted from this activity. The process occurred as a matter of course so that the formal special education referral could be made. Sarah often wondered about the ineffectiveness of her prereferral team. She knew that many of the children referred for special education could in fact succeed in general education classrooms with minor class adjustments. She recognized the resistance of teachers to take advice from the team and the teachers' less than conscientious follow-through. Sarah had never heard of clinical observation. It was not until she began supervising student teachers as a graduate assistant during her masters degree work that she began to understand the value of the clinical supervision cycle and its potential for empowering the Blue Spruce teacher assistance team.

Chapter Outline

Vignette

Chapter Outline

Chapter Content

> *Definition of Clinical Observation*
> *Methods of Data Collection*
> *Considerations for Observer Self-Reflection*

Summary

Vignette Reprise

Portfolio Activities

References

DEFINITION OF CLINICAL OBSERVATION

Clinical observation is a five-step process through which educators can assist each other in collaboratively defining problems, collecting data, and proposing solutions. The process, an adaptation of clinical supervision, is based on a philosophy of mutual respect, personal development, and professional collaboration. Clinical observation can serve as a basic tool for making reflective decisions based on objective data in any of the three collaborative models. When working in the consulting model, the consultant can plan an observation with the teacher, observe in the classroom, and subsequently analyze the data with the teacher. Both can propose needed classroom changes to meet individual student needs. As teachers use the coaching model to support each other in program implementation, they might alternate as observer or observed individual. Together they would plan the observation purpose, analyze the resultant data, and plan personal changes in their professional repertoires. In-school teams, such as TAT's, can take advantage of clinical observation as they attempt to determine needed prereferral strategies for students referred for special education evaluation and services.

Clinical supervision is a cyclical process first proposed as an antidote to routinized teacher appraisal (Cogan, 1973; Goldhammer, Anderson, and Krajewski, 1993). The primary goal of clinical supervision is professional development of the teacher in a nonthreatening environment. Cogan outlined eight steps in the clinical cycle:

- Establishing rapport
- Intensive instructional planning with the teacher

- Planning of the classroom observation with the teacher
- Observing in the classroom
- Analyzing the teaching–learning process
- Planning the post-observation conference strategy
- Conferencing with the teacher
- Resuming planning

The clinical supervisory model stresses teamwork and colleagueship between the supervisor and the teacher. It is supervision for formative development rather than for summative evaluation. Clinical supervision is a process in which the supervisor and supervisee fulfill complementary roles as opposed to traditional superordinate–subordinate positions.

Successful clinical supervisors use an indirect approach, convey concern for the teacher as a person, and promote collaborative problem solving. Such supervision is able to increase teacher morale, as well as productive behavior (Cogan, 1973). Teamwork, indirect and supportive style, and direct help within the classroom, key components of clinical supervision, have been supported by research as impacting on improved classroom teaching behavior (Cooper, 1982; McFaul and Cooper, 1984).

The realities of clinical supervision have been explored by Goldsberry (1984). When asked by school leaders how this process could realistically be implemented in schools, Goldsberry was quick to refer to effective schools literature. Through clinical supervision, norms of colleagueship and experimentation can be fostered. Clinical supervision can lead to collaborative development and implementation of school goals. Goldsberry emphasized five characteristics of clinical supervision that make it more than a mechanical sequence of observations and conferences:

- Relationship of the process to the teacher's individual goals
- The cyclical nature of the process
- The data-based foundation of the process
- Joint interpretation of the observation data
- Renewed hypotheses generation and testing with each cycle

Reciprocity in the process achieved when teachers provide feedback to the supervisor adds strength to clinical supervision and makes the relationship truly collegial.

Karant (1989) has described clinical supervision as a means toward teacher empowerment. She described a mentoring program through which first-year teachers were supervised by senior teachers. During this time, school administrators had minimal responsibility for the novice teachers. Following successful completion of their first year, the novices entered a traditional supervisory tract. Gensante and Matgouranis (1989) reinforced the importance of objective information gained through data collection and nonjudgmental data analysis for success of such a system.

Several concepts have been posed by Krajewski (1984) as necessary in providing a firm foundation for clinical supervision. He described the process as:

- A deliberate intervention into instruction requiring planning what and when to observe, type of analysis to use, and roles of participants
- A creator of productive tension requiring analysis skills, rapport, and time management
- A form of supervision requiring supervisor training
- A goal-oriented and systematic process

As envisioned by Krajewski, the clinical process applies directly to activities of a school-wide prereferral team. Members of such a team must be goal oriented and systematic in planning deliberate interventions in the instruction for at-risk students to prevent the need for more restrictive special educational services and placements.

Instructional supervisors need three kinds of skills—technical, human relations, and managerial (Alfonso, Firth, and Neville, 1984). Technical skill is specialized knowledge and ability. Human relations skill is the ability to work with people and to motivate them. Managerial skill is the ability to make decisions and see relationships. The proportions of the different types of skills in the mix vary according to the supervisor's role in an organization and individual or organizational needs. As a clinical supervisor, technical skills are necessary in order to analyze data and to ask clarifying questions during pre- and post-observation conferences. Human skills are needed especially at the beginning of a relationship in order to build professional rapport, trust, and respect. Managerial skills, especially with regard to time, are necessary throughout a series of clinical cycles.

Although the skill mix is essential in each of the collaboration models, specific applications to individual models are obvious. In the consulting model, technical skills are essential in order for the consultant to share their expertise with fellow professionals. The coaching model demands human skills as individuals alternate the roles of coach and player. Without well-developed human relations skills, a coach might inadvertently insult their collaborative partner. Managerial skills are essential for the teaming model. Teams may involve a large number of individuals whose time and participation must be managed to ensure both effectiveness and efficiency in team functioning.

The importance of collegiality, long-term relationships, and reflection to the clinical supervision process have been documented through several case studies. Nolan, Hawkes, and Francis (1993) found development of a collegial relationship, teacher control over supervisory products, continuity in the process over time, and reflection by both teacher and supervisor to be essential. In one study, postconferences did not become productive until six cycles had been completed. When the supervisor failed to understand the teacher's perspective, the supervisory participants talked to each other but failed to communicate. Reflection on the supervision by both supervisor and teacher was determined to be the "heart" of the postconference.

Clinical supervision has evolved into cognitive coaching (Garmston, Linder, and Whitaker, 1993). Using the cycle, a university observer helped teachers refine lesson objectives in a preconference, observed instruction to collect the data they requested, and guided them in data analysis during the postconference. Through this process, the teachers were empowered to take risks and to continue their own learning. Cognitive coaching fostered reflective skills and collegiality.

Clinical cycles have been found to be productive for pre-service teachers (Meltzer, Trang, and Bailey, 1994). In the teacher education program at Ferrum College, student teachers were responsible for assembling an observation team composed of the mentoring teachers, college supervisor, and a fellow student teacher. The student to be observed provided observers with a description of the lesson, goals/objectives of the lesson, and questions to be answered through the clinical cycle process. Observation data were reviewed and analyzed by the observed student with the observation team. The student teacher also wrote a personal response to the cycle. This process encouraged professional growth of the student teachers more effectively than traditional checklist evaluations. A series of clinical cycles promoted student development through the stages of teacher growth as proposed by Fuller (1969)—from concern about instructional delivery, through concern about task, to concern about learner impact. Confirmation of a job well done provided the incentive for students to work harder at instructional improvement.

Clinical supervision provides a foundation for clinical observation, a basic collaborative tool. The underlying philosophy of teamwork for professional development is consistent with a philosophy for successful educational collaboration. The eight-step process has been condensed to the following five:

- Pre-observation conference
- Observation and data collection
- Data analysis
- Post-observation conference
- Collaborator self-reflection

For maximum benefit, the process should be driven by the person being observed. Clinical observation should facilitate collection of objective data, collaborative analysis of the data, and individual professional reflection. Results can include strategies for program modifications and teachers' professional growth.

METHODS OF DATA COLLECTION

In order to implement clinical observation, the participants must have a repertoire of observation techniques. Methods of collecting data have been categorized in various ways. Acheson and Hansen (1973) describe the many variations of seating chart observational records (SCORe). Through SCORe techniques, a teacher can gain information about the following classroom activity:

- Student at-task behavior
- Verbal flow
- Physical movement
- Individual student activity
- Class response to instruction
- Problem student activity

The observer draws a schema of the classroom. This drawing includes room arrangement in enough detail that the observer can record activity pertinent to the observation goals. The observation data can be as simple or as detailed as the observer and the person being observed desire. Through a SCORe, the observer can record time that an individual student or all students are on task, which students are interacting with whom and their purpose, where and why students are moving about the room, what individual or groups of problem students are doing during a lesson, and physical or verbal interactions between teacher and students.

Figure 3.1 and Figure 3.2 provide two different examples of the use of seating chart observational records. The first figure is a depiction of conversational flow between a teacher and group of nine students. The students were seated in a semicircle around the teacher. After the first lesson, the teacher was not satisfied with the distribution of student talk. Data demonstrated that students who were seated front and center participated in the group discussion more that did students who were seated at the periphery of the semicircle. Wanting to encourage participation by all students, the teacher decided to rearrange students into two smaller semicircles for the second lesson on the following day. The

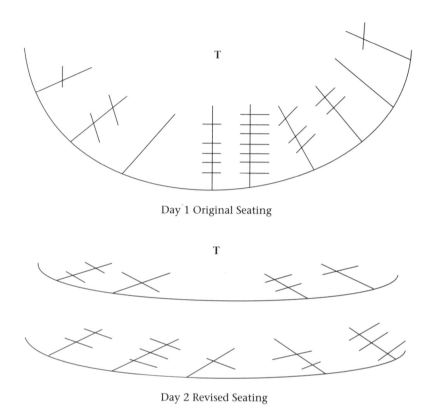

Day 1 Original Seating

T

Day 2 Revised Seating

FIGURE 3.1 SCORe Depiction of Conversational Flow

revised seating seemed to allow a more even flow of conversation and more even distribution of student participation.

The second figure depicts a teacher's movement throughout the room during one lesson period. The classroom was arranged in student pods and activity centers. The twenty-four students were grouped into six pods of four students each. As the teacher conducted a teacher directed lecture, he moved about the room. The free form line recreates his movements. The lines on student desks indicate incidences of off-task behavior. The teacher's path did not include the pod of students seated near the Art Center (Pod 6). This was a group of responsible, self-motivated students. The teacher had not thought that the group needed any prompting to pay attention to the lesson. The data demonstrated otherwise. The members of this pod had far more off-task behavior throughout the lesson than did any of the other groups. After seeing the data, the teacher made a conscious effort to distribute his attention more equally among the students in his class.

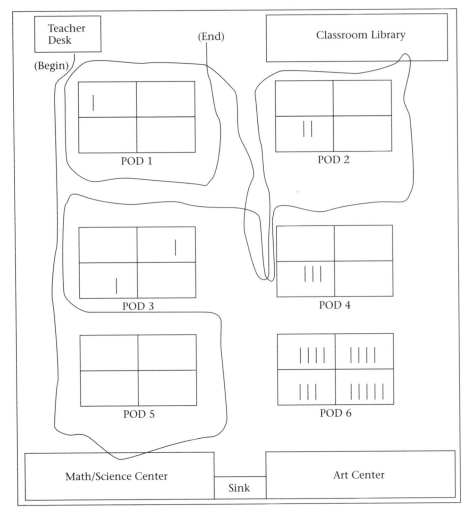

FIGURE 3.2   SCORe Depiction of Teacher Movement

Acheson and Gall (1980) have defined selective verbatim as a form of collecting observational data that can focus on teacher or student talk. The observer records only the type of statements or questions requested. The observer might focus on teacher behavior, such as:

- Teacher questions
- Teacher responses to student questions/statements
- Teacher directions and assignments
- General teacher talk patterns

- Teacher reward and praise statements
- Teacher criticism of pupil behavior
- Teacher control of pupil behavior

On the other hand, the observer might collect data on student behavior, such as:

- Student responses to teacher questions
- Student questions
- Student initiated statements
- General student talk patterns

A third method of collecting data is pattern analysis. The observer records a lesson, transcribes the verbal interactions, numbers each utterance, and looks for patterns. The patterns must be supported by numbered statements and intended or incidental learning inferred. Refer to the appendix at the end of the book as an example of this technique.

Scripting is another data-collection device. The observer attempts to record everything that occurs during the course of the lesson. This record should be nonjudgmental and can be supported by simultaneous video recording.

Any of these techniques may be used in conjunction with traditional behavioral data collection such as:

- Event recording
- Time sampling
- Interval recording
- Duration recording

Event recording involves keeping track of individual classroom events. The lines indicating student off-task behavior in Figure 3.2 are an example of event recording. Recording events every so many minutes, instead of throughout a class period, is an example of time sampling. Time sampling could have been applied to the teacher's movement. What was the teacher doing at five minutes past the hour, at ten minutes past, at fifteen minutes past, and so on? Interval recording involves focusing on a specific behavior and recording its presence at specific intervals of time. For Figure 3.2, the observer might have recorded student attention or inattention every five minutes. Duration recording, on the other hand, record the length of time that a specific behavior continues. Using Pod 6 from Figure 3.2 as an example, the observer might have recorded the length of time that individual students remained off task for each incident of off-task behavior. In addition, anecdotal reports can support the more objective forms of observational data collected and can help to clarify objective data (West, Idol, and Cannon, 1989).

Because there are many ways to collect data, a pre-observation conference is essential to the clinical observation process. During the preconference, the person to be observed should clarify lesson objectives, specify their purpose for the observation, and detail what information they want the observer to collect. Together, the observer and the observee should decide on the best observation data-collection technique to suit their purpose.

CONSIDERATIONS FOR OBSERVER SELF-REFLECTION

Reflective practice of both the observer and person being observed lies at the heart of clinical observation. The teacher's self-reflection is accomplished through postconference observational data analysis. This professional reflection is promoted by the observer presenting nonjudgmental data and probing teacher insight through use of active listening and clarifying questioning. Several forms are presented that can aid clinical observation participants in self-evaluating their part in the process. These forms are exhibited as Figures 3.3, 3.4, 3.5, 3.6, and 3.7.

The first form lists clinical observer competencies (Cooper, Houston, and Warner, 1977). Competencies include assisting teachers in developing interpersonal skills and effective communication with students and others. Teachers should learn to collect and use relevant demographic data about students, the school, and the community. Awareness and understanding of increasing ethnic, cultural, and socioeconomic diversity in individual classrooms has become an essential teaching competency. A clinical observer should be able to guide the teacher in ongoing professional development in areas such as current theory, state-of-the-art teaching methods, assessment, and curricula. Continuous evaluation of the educational environment and classroom management plan will promote students' affective growth. Teachers should be encouraged to maximize their leadership potential and to exploit opportunities for in-class research. Finally, the clinical observer should be perceptive of personal agendas and problems that they are not prepared to address and refer the teacher to appropriate resources for assistance. The observer can use the Clinical Observer Competencies instrument for self-evaluation in each competency area.

Both the observer and the observed professional should be cognizant of interpersonal communication. The underlying philosophy of clinical observation is self-reflection and analysis. Participants in the process must maintain sensitivity to perceptions of each other. The clinical process involves listening, questioning, clarifying, and paraphrasing, rather than telling, assessing, evaluating, or judging. The Communication Evaluation

Rate each statement using the following continuum:

5	4	3	2	1
Strongly Agree	Agree	Undecided	Disagree	Strongly Disagree

1.0   Assist teachers to develop interpersonal skills and effective communication with students, colleagues, and school constituencies.

_____1.1   Describe factors affecting communication between individuals or groups of people.

_____1.2   Demonstrate interpersonal communication skills.

2.0   Assist teachers to gather and utilize relevant data about school, classroom, and community environments.

_____2.1   Identify and use appropriate sociodemographic data collection techniques to gather data related to school, classroom, and community environments.

_____2.2   Help teachers interpret and utilize sociodemographic data about school, classroom, and community environments.

3.0   Assist teachers to understand and work effectively with different socioeconomic/ethnic/cultural groups.

_____3.1   Identify various value positions and behavior patterns of ethnic/cultural and socioeconomic groups attending our schools.

_____3.2   Help teachers develop more positive relationships with members of ethnic/cultural and socioeconomic groups attending our schools.

4.0   Assist teachers to translate knowledge of current educational research and development into instructional practices.

_____4.1   Identify sources that report research findings relevant to instruction.

_____4.2   Interpret research findings so that teachers can understand the instructional implications.

5.0   Assist teachers to develop a personal teaching style consistent with their own philosophy.

_____5.1   Understand different models of teaching and their underlying philosophies.

_____5.2   Help teachers analyze their own teaching styles and compare them with different models of teaching.

6.0   Assist teachers to improve their understanding of basic curricular concepts and theories.

_____6.1   Explain the scope and sequence of curricula taught in the subject matter area or grade level.

_____6.2   Explain the various philosophical positions of curricular programs taught in the subject matter area or grade level.

7.0   Assist teachers to understand and use techniques and instruments designed to diagnose students' academic and social development needs.

_____7.1   Identify major tests and instruments that are useful in diagnosing students' academic and social development.

_____7.2   Administer formal diagnostic instruments and interpret their results.

8.0   Assist teachers to design, develop, and maintain environments that facilitate learning.

_____8.1   Describe procedures for establishing and maintaining a healthy and safe physical environment in the classroom.

_____8.2   Describe classroom environmental factors that facilitate learning.

FIGURE 3.3   Clinical Observer Competencies

From Cooper, J.M., Houston, W.R., and Warner, A.R. (1977). *S.B.T.E. Self-Assessment Instrument*. Houston: University of Houston College of Education. Reprinted with permission.

(continued)

9.0   Assist teachers to develop instructional goals and objectives.
_____9.1   Derive and define instructional objectives based on the educational goals of the school.
_____9.2   Analyze classroom procedures to identify hidden or incidental objectives.
10.0   Assist teachers to develop and/or adapt instructional programs and materials.
_____10.1   Modify instructional materials without distorting the purpose of the materials.
_____10.2   Organize a curriculum to provide a variety of methods and materials from which students can make choices in the planning of their educational experiences.
11.0   Assist teachers to select and utilize various strategies and models of teaching.
_____11.1   Describe various models of teaching, their application strategies, theoretical backgrounds, and research findings.
_____11.2   Help other teachers to use these models in their classrooms.
12.0   Assist teachers to design and implement personalized learning plans.
_____12.1   Recognize and describe individual personalities and learning styles.
_____12.2   Develop and demonstrate individualized learning plans.
13.0   Assist teachers to develop effective leadership skills.
_____13.1   Use various techniques to help a group of teachers build group cohesion, interact with one another, and stay on task.
_____13.2   Model appropriate use of various leadership styles.
14.0   Assist teachers to understand and use effective techniques of classroom management.
_____14.1   Differentiate between classroom instructional problems and classroom managerial problems.
_____14.2   Describe the nature and dynamics of various approaches to classroom management.
15.0   Evaluate instructional effectiveness by collecting, analyzing, and interpreting data on teacher and student behavior.
_____15.1   Utilize a variety of observational techniques to collect, analyze, and interpret classroom data on teacher performance.
_____15.2   Help teachers identify congruencies between their intent and their action.
16.0   Assist teachers to develop, implement, and assess continuing individual professional growth plans.
_____16.1   Help teachers identify discrepancies between their ideal professional status and their current status.
_____16.2   Help teachers to develop growth plans for reducing the discrepancies between their current professional status and their ideal one.
17.0   Plan and conduct individual conferences with teachers.
_____17.1   Establish open communication with the teachers.
_____17.2   Ask clarifying questions and paraphrase the teacher's ideas.
18.0   Recognize the existence of personal problems that affect a teacher's instructional effectiveness and initiate appropriate referral process.
_____18.1   Refer a teacher to several sources of assistance that can help in solving the teacher's personal problems.
_____18.2   Recognize when teaching problems may be related to personal problems.
19.0   Facilitate research studies on teaching and learning.
_____19.1   Develop studies to help solve teaching problems.
_____19.2   Interpret and use results of studies.

FIGURE 3.3   *Continued*

Rate each question using the following continuum:

5	4	3	2	1
Always	Usually	Sometimes	Seldom	Never

_____ 1. Do I remain silent after I ask a question so that the teacher with whom I am interacting can respond?

_____ 2. Do I frown or grimace (show disapproval) when the teacher with whom I am interacting responds to a question I have asked?

_____ 3. Do I smile to indicate approval of responses?

_____ 4. Do I encourage continuous verbal responses by nodding my head?

_____ 5. Do I maintain eye contact appropriately while interacting with a teacher?

_____ 6. Do I narrow the distance between myself and my teacher to maintain psychological proximity (a sense of closeness) while I am communicating?

_____ 7. Do I use hand and arm movements to emphasize important points and to reinforce verbal statements?

_____ 8. Do I recognize and respond positively to quizzical, contemplative, or frustration behaviors by teachers?

_____ 9. Do I respond judgmentally to comments made by the teachers?

_____10. Do I violate territorial boundaries of the teacher?

_____11. Do I use appropriate vocal intonation and inflection levels when interacting with a teacher?

_____12. Do I deal with specifics in a concrete fashion when I respond to a teacher?

_____13. Do I use clarification processes during an interaction with a teacher?

_____14. Do I respond to feelings being expressed by a teacher?

_____15. Do I arrange space in such a way that it is conducive to positive interactions with teachers?

_____16. Do I show respect for a teacher during an interaction?

_____17. Do I appear rushed and unable to spend adequate time dealing with a teacher's problems?

_____18. Do I appear observant of my teacher's nonverbal cues?

_____19. Do I respond appropriately to the teacher's nonverbal cues?

_____20. Do I allow my teacher sufficient time to present his/her position in its entirety before I begin to react to the problem?

_____21. Do I appear to intimidate my teacher with the kinds of questions I ask?

FIGURE 3.4   Communication Evaluation Form

From Cooper, J.M., Houston, W.R., and Warner, A.R. (1977). *S.B.T.E. Self-Assessment Instrument.* Houston: University of Houston College of Education. Reprinted with permission.

Form can assist process participants in maintaining appropriate forms of communication.

The Communication Evaluation Form directs a clinical observer to assess their own nonverbal and verbal behavior. Nonverbal behaviors include arrangement of space, facial expressions, and gestures. Persons involved in this process should arrange a comfortable, nonthreatening

The observer will encourage the teacher to:

- Describe the lesson to be observed.
- Describe what s/he will be doing during the lesson.
- Describe expected student behaviors.
- Predict potential problems, weak points, and concerns.
- Agree upon the observer's role. What will be observed and what data will be collected?

Conference Analysis

1. Did the teacher state the objectives?   yes__no__
2. Were the objectives expressed in observable terms?   yes__no__
3. Did you restate the objectives?   yes__no__
4. Briefly list the objectives.

5. Did you discuss the strategy?   yes__no__
6. Were other strategy options discussed?   yes__no__
7. What teaching techniques were planned?

8. Did the teacher select the instruments?   yes__no__
9. What instruments were selected?

10. Which objectives will the instruments provide data about?

11. Were other observation techniques discussed?   yes__no__

FIGURE 3.5   Pre-Observation Conference Form

From Acheson, K.A., and Hansen, J.H. (1973). *Classroom Observations and Conferencing with Teachers.* Tallahassee, FL: T.I.P.S. Reprinted with permission.

atmosphere conducive to professional discussion. Pre- and post-observation conferences in a comfortable setting between two or more mutually respectful participants will promote effective collaboration.

Verbal behavior includes both what is said and how it is communicated. For collaboration in any form to be successful, the participants

The observer will:

- Provide the teacher with data.
- Elicit feelings, inferences and opinions.
- Ask clarifying questions.
- Listen more and talk less.
- Acknowledge and paraphrase the teacher's statements.
- Avoid giving direct advice.
- Provide specific communication about performance and growth.
- Provide opportunities for practice and comparison.
- Elicit alternative techniques and explanations.

Post-Conference Self-Analysis Sheet

1. Statements that directed the teacher to analyze objective data.

2. Statements that asked you for an opinion.

3. Teacher statements in which you were asked for data about the lesson. Star those to which you did respond with data.

4. Statements that contain specific data from the observation instruments.

5. Verbatim excerpts demonstrating:

   Observer/Teacher

   Providing data

   Seeking inferences

   Seeking opinions

   Seeking feelings

FIGURE 3.6   Post-Observation Conference Form

Adapted from Acheson, K.A., and Hansen, J.H. (1973). *Classroom Observation and Conferencing with Teachers.* Tallahassee, FL: T.I.P.S. Reprinted with permission.

(continued)

6. How many questions were asked by each person:

   Observer/Teacher

   About data from previous observations?

   To clarify what the other person said?

   About teaching in general?

   About other issues (please specify)?

7. How many suggestions were made by each person?

   Observer/Teacher

   About the causes of previously observed classroom events?

   About alternative approaches for the future?

   About other matters (please specify)?

8. Who talked more?   Who talked less?

   Was this distribution appropriate?

   Explain.

9. What will you do differently during the next observation cycle as a result of your analysis?

FIGURE 3.6   *Continued*

1. Did you regard the conference as being helpful?
2. What were the most effective aspects of the observation and conference?
3. What were the least effective?
4. Rate each of the following behaviors on frequency and helpfulness.

Frequency	5	4	3	2	1
	Often	Usually	Sometimes	Seldom	Never
Helpful	5	4	3	2	1
	Extremely	Very	Adequately	Rather	Not

F____ H____ Acknowledged and showed understanding of what I said.
F____ H____ Sought further clarification of what I said.
F____ H____ Avoided making decisions for me.
F____ H____ Asked about my feelings.
F____ H____ Dealt with objectives, strategies, and techniques.
F____ H____ Gave specific praise for observed growth.
F____ H____ Let me talk.
F____ H____ Gave me objective information about my teaching.
F____ H____ Helped me to identify problems and plan several alternative solutions
F____ H____ Encouraged me to draw inferences from observational data.
F____ H____ Used observational systems to collect needed and useful information.
F____ H____ Translated abstract concerns into observable behaviors.
F____ H____ Concentrated on the most relevant aspects of teaching.
F____ H____ Helped me plan a variety of teaching techniques.
F____ H____ Aided me in applying varied viewpoints to explain classroom occurrences.

FIGURE 3.7   Teacher Conference Analysis Form
Adapted from Acheson, K.A., and Hansen, J.H. (1973). *Classroom Observation and Conferencing with Teachers*. Tallahassee, FL: T.I.P.S. Reprinted with permission.

must actively listen to each other. Active listening is indicated by eye contact, an interested expression, and positive body postures. Active listening results in clarification through paraphrasing. It is imperative that parties to collaboration not become entangled in semantic misunderstandings. Active listening encourages each collaborator to empathize with the others and to try to understand the purpose of their collaboration through the others' perspectives. Because successful collaborators actively listen to the positions and concerns of each other, they are able to facilitate self-directed problem solutions, rather than judging past performance and dictating what should be done in the future.

Effective interpersonal feedback has been described by Friend and Cook (1996). Characteristics of effective feedback include the following:

• Feedback is descriptive, not evaluative.
• Feedback is specific.

- Feedback is directed toward a changeable situation or behavior.
- Feedback is concise.

Basing feedback on objective data collected during the observation phase of a clinical observation cycle, and encouraging the observee to analyze and reflect on the data, promote the above characteristics of effective feedback. The data would promote descriptive, specific, and concise feedback and would allow for self-directed situational or behavioral change. The Communication Evaluation Form is a tool for promoting self-reflection with regard to both nonverbal and verbal forms of communication.

Often in this cyclical process, the post observation conference from one observation becomes the pre observation conference for the next. The Pre- and Post-Observation Conference Forms serve as guides to maintain participants' focus. The Pre-Observation Conference Form outlines the overall purpose of the conference and leads the observer through an analysis of personal conference performance. Similarly, the Post-Observation Conference Form assists the observer in maintaining the conference purpose and in analyzing personal adeptness at conference implementation. Each clinical observation cycle should maintain one specific purpose. As a result of a cycle, the initial purpose may be expanded, modified, or resolved. Recording of conference notes allows the process to continue on track, and fosters participants' continuing growth through the collaboration.

The final form, Teacher Conference Analysis, allows the observed teacher to evaluate professional benefit of the post-observation conference. Because positive personal interaction is essential for successful clinical observation, both self-reflection and objective feedback are important components of the process. The final form allows the observed teacher to provide feedback to the observer, and serves as a final check to the system by ensuring that the process does indeed represent a collaborative effort rather than being observer controlled and driven.

Because this process is defined by the following characteristics, clinical observation serves as a basic tool in any form of collaboration.

- Clinical observation is a means for collecting objective data through which current practice can by assessed and needed modifications can be determined.
- The foundation of clinical observation is formative teacher development for continuing professional growth resulting in positive student outcomes.
- The data collection and analysis process is driven by the person seeking assistance in collaboration with the data collector.

- The clinical observation cycle occurs in an environment of professional equity, respect, and trust.

SUMMARY

This chapter has introduced clinical observation as philosophically compatible with and as an essential tool for collaborative practice. The five steps in the process have been outlined. Ways to collect data and methods of self-analysis as both observer and observee have been described.

VIGNETTE REPRISE

Had the Blue Spruce TAT used clinical observation, their activities might have been more than an exercise in futility. Because the process of conference–observation–conference was conducted superficially, it was ineffective. Had the TAT met with a referring teacher in a collaborative preconference based on mutual trust to determine observation objectives, the observations may have resulted in useful data. Had the postconference been based on mutual respect between TAT and teacher, data analysis might have resulted in collaborative dialogue with both parties gaining insight into the classroom teaching–learning interchange, proposing alternative strategies, and agreeing on implementation and evaluation plans. Because their own opinions were valued, teachers would not resent advice from the TAT. With its basis in professional respect, objectivity, and support, clinical observation enhances any professional collaborative effort.

PORTFOLIO ACTIVITIES

1. *Personal Application:* Conduct a clinical observation cycle with a peer as either the observer or the observed.

   Keep a log of each part of the observation cycle.
   - Preconference
   - Observation and data collection
   - Data analysis
   - Post-observation conference
   - Self-reflection

2. *Professional Reflection:* Describe the prereferral process that you have experienced. Analyze the effectiveness or ineffectiveness of the process. How would you change your prereferral process to increase its effectiveness?

3. *Action Research:* With a peer, develop a professional development plan for the next year. Include the focus of improvement, method of peer observation, schedule of interactions, and criterion for goal achievement. Consider the five components of action research—purpose and process, data collection and analysis, outside support needed, interested audience, and possible side effects.

REFERENCES

Acheson, K.A., and Gall, M.D. (1980). *Techniques in the Clinical Supervision of Teachers.* New York: Longman Publishers.

Acheson, K.A., and Hansen, J.H. (1973). *Classroom Observation and Conferencing with Teachers.* Tallahassee, FL: T.I.P.S.

Alfonso, R.J., Firth, G., and Neville, R. (1984). "The Supervisory Skill Mix." *Educational Leadership* 41(7): 16–18.

Cogan, M.L. (1973). *Clinical Supervision.* Boston: Houghton Mifflin Co.

Cooper, J.M. (1982). "Supervision of Teachers." In H.E. Mitzel (ed.), *Encyclopedia of Educational Research,* 5th ed. New York: The Free Press.

Cooper, J.M., Houston, W.R., and Warner, A.R. (1977). *S.B.T.E. Self-Assessment Instrument.* Houston: University of Houston College of Education.

Friend, M., and Cook, L. (1996). *Interactions: Collaboration Skills for School Professionals,* 2d ed. White Plains, NY: Longman Publishers.

Fuller, F.F. (1969). "Concerns of Teachers: A Developmental Conceptualization." *American Educational Research Journal* 6: 207–226.

Garmston, R., Linder, C., and Whitaker, J. (1993). "Reflections on Cognitive Coaching." *Educational Leadership* 51(2): 57–61.

Gensante, L.J., and Matgouranis, E.M. (1989). "The More I See, the Better I Teach." *Educational Leadership* 46(8): 28.

Goldhammer, R., Anderson, R., and Krajewski, R. (1993). *Clinical Supervision: Special Methods for the Supervision of Teachers,* 3d ed. New York: Holt, Rinehart, and Winston.

Goldsberry, L.F. (1984). "The Realities of Clinical Supervision." *Educational Leadership* 41(7): 12–15.

Karant, V.I. (1989). "Supervision in the Age of Teacher Empowerment." *Educational Leadership* 46(8): 27–29.

Krajewski, R.J. (1984). "No Wonder It Didn't Work!" *Educational Leadership* 41(7): 11.

McFaul, S.A., and Cooper, J.M. (1984). "Peer Clinical Supervision: Theory vs. Reality." *Educational Leadership* 41(7): 4–9.

Meltzer, J., Trang, M., and Bailey, B. (1994). "Clinical Cycles: A Productive Tool for Teacher Education." *Phi Delta Kappan* 75(8): 613–619.

Nolan, J., Hawkes, B., and Francis, P. (1993). "Case Studies: Windows onto Clinical Supervision." *Educational Leadership* 51(2): 52–56.

West, J.F., Idol, L., and Cannon, G. (1989). *Collaboration in the Schools.* Austin, TX: Pro-Ed.

4

THE CONSULTING MODEL

Vignette

In order to help pay the added expenses of full-time graduate study and minimally offset her loss of income while in school, Sarah applied for a work-study position at the university. The College of Education and Human Services had been awarded a five-year Projects with Industry Grant by the federal government. The purpose of the grant was provision of supported employment opportunities for persons with severe disabilities. Sarah was excited for the chance to learn more about post-school employment for special education students. Plainsview, where she was attending graduate school, seemed to hold a wealth of opportunities not available in Sarah's small home community. She was hoping to be able to apply this experience on a smaller scale in Blue Spruce when she returned home. In order to gain the experience she needed, Sarah became Marissa's job coach.

Marissa was a young woman with severe developmental delays and many autistic-like behaviors. Although she dressed similarly to her eighteen-year-old peers in jeans and tee shirts, she was overweight and often forgot to wash her hair. She would graduate from high school in the spring with skills as a domestic that she had acquired in her work-study program over the last four years. Marissa hoped to work in a local motel as a maid. Sarah, as her high school job coach, would act as a consultant to the motel manager and the lead housekeeper. She would help them learn to prompt Marissa in her daily routine of punching a time clock, changing the beds, and scouring the bathrooms in ten suites. They would have to cue Marissa when it was her break time and when she must return to work. Sarah would be a resource to the motel staff during the first six months of Marissa's employment as she gradually faded from her role in Marissa's life.

Chapter Outline

DEFINITION OF THE CONSULTING MODEL

An expert giving advice to a novice exemplifies the consulting model. This has been a traditional collaborative model in special education for nearly twenty years, since the passage of P.L. 94-142. Perhaps the best explanation of the model is provided by Idol, Paolucci-Whitcomb, and Nevin (1987) in the first edition of *Collaborative Consultation.* They define consultation as a triad in which the consultant (special education teacher) provides advice to a mediator (general education teacher) for the benefit of a target (student). This approach is an indirect service delivery model. The consultant does not work directly with the student but provides the information and resources necessary for successful service delivery. The consulting model is defined by the inequality of those involved. One party has more expertise, knowledge, or experience than the other in a specific area. The other party relies on the expert for information and guidance to develop competence in the area of need.

EXAMPLES OF THE CONSULTING MODEL

Examples of the consulting model discussed in this chapter fall into the following three subcategories: mentor teacher programs, student support efforts, and interagency consultation. Mentor teacher programs refer to master teachers serving as guides for their apprentices or protégés who are novices in the teaching profession. Much of this chapter is devoted to the concept of mentoring as collaboration in the form of consulting. As teachers hone their pedagogical skills to provide for student diversity, they will have to mentor each other. General and special education teachers have different but complementary skills. They should consult with each other for skill development.

Student support efforts involve special educational consultation for general educators who are including students with special educational needs in their general education classes. Although there is some discussion of using consulting for student support, the discussion is not expansive. The role of special education teacher as consultant to general education teachers has been well documented and extensively described. Consulting for student support remains a valid use of the consulting model but should be used with discretion in an age of increasing inclusive educational practice.

Interagency examples of consultation demonstrate interaction between and among educational and other human services organizations on behalf of individuals with disabilities. The concept of wraparound service to students as clients is a new but growing concept. Because schools and human service agencies are just waking up to their mutual need for collaboration, the discussion of school–agency collaboration in the form of consulting is brief.

Mentor Teacher Programs as a Form of Consulting

The consulting model of collaboration is exemplified in mentor teacher programs. Mentors are not consultants in the traditional sense of an outside expert called on for technical assistance on a specific issue at one point in time. Rather, mentors are consultants in the best sense. A mentor is a guide offering expert assistance and professional support over an extended period of time.

Mentors serve as "experts" to beginning teachers, who are in an apprenticeship role. First-year teachers require assistance with basics, such as school policies, administrative expectations, building community awareness, and developing parental rapport. Beyond day-to-day survival skills, new teachers often seek affirmation of their instructional strategies, advice on dealing with student behavioral challenges, and suggestions for successfully running the appraisal gamut. Having experienced professionals mentor the inexperienced has been found to cushion the shock most new teachers encounter as they leave their university methods classes and attempt to implement theory in the public schools.

Irvine (1985) looked at perceptions of beginning and master teachers with regard to their roles. She found that beginning teachers expect maximum support during their first few months, but that their need for support diminishes over time. For her project, Irvine assigned ten novice teachers to master teachers at the beginning of the school year. The beginning teachers completed a questionnaire addressing their expectations of the mentor. The questionnaire listed forty-six different mentor teacher responsibilities. In September, the novices expected their mentors to be responsible for forty-three of the forty-six tasks. Their needs included assistance with instruction, classroom management, planning, record keeping, and parent conferencing. By February, their expectations had been reduced to ten tasks, all addressing the beginners' continuing need for support, communication, advice, information, and reinforcement.

Master teachers reported on the value of their training in active listening, helping skills, role playing, and simulations. They felt that assertiveness training would be helpful for their role. Master teachers' concerns included the need for more released time in order to fulfill their responsibilities and to schedule conferences with their novice. As a result of participation in the program, the mentors had re-analyzed their own teaching and had been "rejuvenated" by the novice teachers' enthusiasm. However, they expressed the opinion that not every teacher could be a mentor.

California implemented a state-wide mentor teacher program (Wagner, 1985). According to the state plan, mentors were appointed for one-, two-, or three-year terms to work with teacher trainees, beginning teachers, and other teachers as needed. Mentors had to be licensed teachers with tenure, had to have recent classroom experience, and had to demonstrate "exemplary" teaching. The state legislative guidelines designated mentor responsibilities as assisting and guiding new teachers, providing staff development for teachers, and developing curricula. Mentors were not to evaluate teachers. Other than these general regulations, local schools were left to their own discretion in developing district mentor programs. The five most common mentor responsibilities were found to be staff development or consultation with individual teachers, school or district level staff development, locating and organizing curricular materials, curriculum development, and assistance to beginning teachers.

Wagner (1985) has described one California district's successful efforts. A large district in the Los Angeles area had an instructional resource teacher (IRT) program in place when the state approved mentor programs. The district combined the two by defining IRT functions as those performed on-site at a school and mentor functions as district-wide. Successful program applicants had to demonstrate exemplary communication and teaching skills, ability to prepare and deliver workshops, leadership, and trustworthiness. Candidates who passed the initial screening process were interviewed and asked to submit a videotape of their teaching.

Following selection as a mentor, candidates participated in district training including adult learning theory, curriculum implementation, instructional methodology, peer observation, and coaching. The newly trained mentors formulated specific assignments and developed district interest in their focus area. With the IRTs, mentors formed school mentor instructional resource teams (MIRTs) to provide requested curricular, instructional, and management assistance and coaching. District-wide, mentors demonstrated model lessons, training, and classroom observation and coaching. In this district, the mentor teacher program was viewed as a way to provide leadership opportunities for teachers and to retain masters in the teaching profession.

Another California district initiated a training effort combining theory, demonstration, practice, feedback, and coaching in order to help new teachers (Moffett, St. John, and Isken, 1987). Concerned with teacher turnover in light of the need to implement complex curricula, the district developed a mentor program to help new teachers transition from academia to the classroom. The program was based on three premises:

- Teachers develop style early in their careers, so support for a professional style consistent with district philosophy is essential for beginning teachers.
- Following presentation of content with demonstration, practice, and individual help will result in application of new teaching skills.
- Teachers assisting each other at an individual school site will build a support system encouraging continued teaching improvement.

The basis of this program is consistent with the work of Joyce and Showers (1982; 1983; Joyce and Weil, 1986; Joyce, Weil, and Showers, 1992) who advocate theory to practice with peer assistance as teachers learn new teaching models. They have found that demonstration alone during an in-service presentation rarely results in continued practice of pedagogical innovations over time. Individual practice of a new teaching technique under the guidance and support of a peer, however, substantially increases the probability that the technique will become part of the teacher's regular teaching repertoire.

Six essential elements forming the foundation of this California mentor program included new teacher training, recruitment and training of peer mentors, released time or stipends for training, practice and application, pairing mentors with new teachers, and observations. Training involved a full week in the fall and two or three additional staff development days including a mid-year follow-up session in which additional skill content was taught and motivational speakers were featured. Recruitment and training of the mentors was as important as new teacher training. Not all teachers would feel comfortable in the role of a mentor. Some experienced teachers were not able to commit to the extra time involved with the mentoring program. Pairing of mentors and teachers was an especially important and delicate aspect of the program. Matching new teachers with mentors who were compatible both personally and philosophically was not always possible, but doing so prevented unnecessary conflict and supported positive mentoring relationships. In-class observations were an important part of the program. The clinical observation preconference–observation–postconference sequence with data analysis and mentor self-reflection was an invaluable program tool.

New teachers responded positively to the training. Instructional training provided them with an avenue for thinking and talking about effective teaching. Emphasis on positive reinforcement helped them manage their classes effectively. The novice teachers viewed their mentors as colleagues to whom they could turn with doubts and frustrations. Mentors were helpful, understanding, and available. Through this program, the district was able to provide support for new teachers, preventing isolation and increasing competence.

Mentor teachers played a role in the Charlotte-Mecklenburg career development plan (Hanes and Mitchell, 1985). The overall program involved an initial training and practice period of several years. New teachers progressed through four steps:

- Provisional teacher—the first step involving carefully supervised practice
- Career nominee—the second step involving planned study of philosophical and theoretical bases
- Career candidate—the third step involving development of professional skills at the school or district level
- Career level—the fourth step indicating professional teaching performance

Career development thus began with individual competence. The provisional teacher was given the chance to demonstrate personal professional development as an instructor in the classroom through close supervision. Having demonstrated initial competence as a novice, the teacher's continued growth was supported through continuing education as a career nominee. Competent individuals showing commitment to lifelong learning were given the opportunity to expand their professional role beyond the classroom to activity at the district level. Finally, teachers who continued to meet the standards of each previous level were recognized as career level professionals. Their work at this level did not necessarily take them out of the classroom, but career level teachers were recognized for their expanded professional roles with school-wide and district-level responsibilities.

Mentors played an important part in staff development. They were released from teaching one-half day per month in order to work with new teachers. A mentor taught in the same subject area or grade level as their provisional teacher. They were role models for effective teaching, had to communicate effectively, served as observers, advisors, counselors, and evaluators. Mentors came to understand the importance of building rapport and trust, of constructive confrontation, and of achieving balance between formative and summative evaluation. Novice teachers ranked opportunity for informal conversation, help with management of student behavior, advice on instructional presentation, and assistance with time management as among the more important functions of their mentors.

Part of the Charlotte-Mecklenburg career development plan were elaborate evaluation procedures (Schlechty, 1985). The evaluation system combined formative and summative evaluation as means of improving practice and of making personnel decisions. The evaluation purposes included the following:

- Communicating performance expectations
- Providing feedback to teachers with regard to these expectations
- Providing data with regard to the quality of district training, assistance, and support
- Providing data for making informed personnel decisions

The evaluation system distinguished between competencies and expectations. Beginning teachers were evaluated on competence, that is, whether or not they demonstrated skill, but experienced teachers were evaluated on the expectation that they demonstrated skill routinely and consistently. Areas in which teachers were evaluated included classroom performance, faculty performance, and professional performance. Observers/evaluators were responsible for carrying out the system. Five guiding principles included:

- Continuous evaluation
- Multiple criteria for evaluation

- Multiple evaluators
- Long-term evaluation for personnel decisions
- Regular evaluation of the evaluation process itself

Continuous, self-regulated evaluation procedures maintained program quality. Multiple criteria reviewed by multiple evaluators permitted a comprehensive view of performance from more than one perspective. Considering the evaluation history of an individual before making personnel decisions promoted fair employment practices.

Observers/evaluators served as consultants or mentors throughout the evaluation process. They were drawn from a cadre of career level teachers and remained in the role for a maximum of two years at a time. The observer/evaluator visited the classroom of any teacher in the career development program to compile, analyze, describe, and rate the teacher in five areas:

- Management of instructional time
- Management of student behavior
- Instructional presentation
- Monitoring
- Feedback

A narrative description of classroom practice provided the rationale for ratings.

Another form of mentoring in this process was advisory/assessment teams. Together with an advisory/assessment team, teachers developed action-growth plans. These plans provided a strategy for beginning teacher improvement in competencies and emphasized performance goals as the teacher progressed through the career development program. In addition to developing action-growth plans, the teams assessed observation reports, summarized data, and recommended career or salary advancement.

Sweeney and Manatt (1984) described a similar system for supervising marginal teachers. Effective teaching was defined as teaching to an objective, designing learning activities to reach the objective, efficient and effective lesson delivery, assessing student mastery, providing for enrichment or remediation, and promoting a positive learning environment. The system for evaluating teacher performance was developed both to provide the teacher with time and help to improve performance, but also to provide the school with sufficient data for making difficult personnel decisions if necessary. When an individual's teaching was assessed as less than satisfactory, the intensive assistance team went into action. The team was composed of three or four staff members willing to provide assistance to the teacher. The team's role was neither for evaluating, nor for evidence gathering. As the team coordinated teacher observations, team meetings and dialogue with the teacher, the school administrator maintained a status report of the assistance team process. The report included dates, status reports, summaries, composites, reviews, and documentation sources. Ultimately, administrators had to make a decision to discontinue assistance, to continue assistance, or to consider dismissal. The intensive assistance team served in the consulting model to mentor individual teacher efforts to improve teaching performance.

The research on mentoring was synthesized by Gray and Gray (1985). They found that mentors serve five career functions for protégés:

- Exposing protégés to opportunities
- Coaching
- Sponsoring
- Protecting
- Challenging

Psychosocial functions of mentors include:

- Role modeling
- Counseling
- Affirming
- Befriending

Of the eight possible mentor roles identified, the most frequent included:

- Teacher
- Confidant
- Role model
- Talent developer
- Sponsor
- Opportunity provider
- Protector
- Leader

These career functions, psychosocial functions, and roles are not those normally associated with consulting. A traditional understanding of consulting is an outside expert with little ownership of a situation coming to assist with acute problems. Mentoring, on the other hand, involves a close relationship between the mentor and the protégé. The mentor protects, affirms, and serves as a confidant. The mentor is a consultant, however, by the fact of being more informed and experienced than the individual being mentored. The mentor is an expert advising the novice in areas of need.

The mentor's relationship with their novice teacher progresses through several stages. Initiation refers to beginning the relationship when both mentor and apprentice attempt to portray their best. As the relationship develops, mentor and protégé cultivate their professional friendship. Gradually, the protégé becomes disillusioned with the mentor as he/she gains professional independence and no longer needs the mentor's guidance. The two may separate or part ways until their relationship is redefined and transformed into a more equal professional partnership.

Figure 4.1 shows the dynamics of the mentor–protégé relationship as it changes over time. The capital or lower case M refers to the mentor, while the capital or lower case P refers to the protégé. Capital and lower case letters are used to denote weight of responsibility. Early in the relationship, professional responsibility lies with the mentor (capital M), while the protégé (small p) is learning his or her role. As the relationship develops and the protégé grows professionally, responsibility gradually shifts from the mentor (small m) to the protégé (capital P). When the protégé matures, he or she becomes the professional equal of the mentor. As this occurs, the collaborative relationship moves from the consulting model to that of coaching (Chapter 5) or teaming (Chapter 6).

Consulting in the form of mentoring serves novice professionals. New teachers can rely on their more experienced mentors to guide them through the first few difficult years of teaching. The mentor is an expert teacher and as such provides both technical assistance and moral support to his or her protégé. As the novice develops professionally, the relationship develops into a form where the technical assistance and support are mutually given between professional equals.

Consulting for Student Support

A second form of the consulting model appearing in professional literature is consulting for student support. This has been a common form of the model since the passage of special education mandates and even before that. Teachers with expertise in areas of student need serve as consultants to teachers who work with the student in mainstream educational settings. As a consultant, a special educator serves as a resource to general education teachers. In such a role the teacher is expected to maintain a caseload of students who are seen on a regular basis, in addition to serving as a classroom consultant for their students as well as for others who demonstrate similar educational needs.

Responsible	M	Mp	MP	mP	P
Mentor Role					
Leadership	M tells p	M sells p	M invites P	m delegates to P	P is self-directed
Role model	p observes M	M teaches p	M and P dialogue	m supports P	P "fits in"
Instructor	M instructs p	M queries p	M facilitates P	P synthesizes	P self-instructs
Demonstrator	M exemplifies	M shows p	M and P demonstrate	m supports P	P demonstrates
Motivator	M is enthusiastic	M enculturates p	M and P contract	m encourages P	P has own values
Supervisor	M directs p	M suggests to p	M and P brainstorm	m gives feedback	P self-evaluates
Counselor	M provides cases	M confronts p	M and P contract	m listens to P	P resolves problems
Promoter	M arranges for p	M prepares p	M and P discuss	m helps P	P internalizes

FIGURE 4.1   Mentor–Protégé Relationship Progression

From Gray, W.A., and Gray, M.M. (1985). "Synthesis of Research on Mentoring Beginning Teachers." *Educational Leadership* 43(3): 37–43. Reprinted with permission of the Association for Supervision and Curriculum Development. Copyright © 1985 by ASCD. All rights reserved.

In Chapter 1, several texts were discussed that specifically address the special educator's consultant role. Wiederholt, Hammill, and Brown (1983) provided a guide for preparing resource room consultant teachers. Sugai and Tindal (1993) have provided a behavioral approach to consultation. The educational consultant's role has been elaborated upon by Heron and Harris (1993), as well as by Idol (1993) in handbooks for consultants. Perhaps the most complete guide for special education consultants is the first edition of *Collaborative Consultation* by Idol, Paolucci-Whitcomb, and Nevin (1987).

Mainstream consultation in secondary settings has been found to be an effective way to keep students with disabilities in general education settings (Tindal, Shinn, Walz, and Germann, 1987). Consultation specialists worked with teachers to change the general education environment. Mainstream consultation agreements (MCA) delineated mainstream teacher expectations, set criteria for student assessment and attainment, and defined responsibilities of the student, mainstream teacher, and consultant. Through this program, special education teachers supported general education teachers who initially expected students to fail their content area course. The result was student success.

Brief strategic intervention (BSI) (Amatea, 1990) is another example of the consulting model of collaboration used for student support. School counselors have used BSI to identify key elements in behavioral problems, formulate a solution shift from original solution efforts, develop specific action steps for new ways of responding, and monitor the change efforts, all in an effort to help teachers deal with problematic student behavior. This consultation strategy was based on the premise that it is often an adult (teacher, parent, or other) whose responses maintain a child's problem behavior. BSI assumes that problems are the result of mishandled situations rather than faulty learning or pathology. Using information to design a change message, the counselor, as a consultant, delivered change messages to the teacher in a nonauthoritarian manner through tentatively made suggestions or questions.

The consulting model has been successfully employed to integrate students with severe disabilities into general education settings (Janney and Meyer, 1990). Fifteen students were targeted who had returned from segregated settings or who had never been enrolled in their neighborhood schools. The directors of this project matched consultants to students. The student's teacher worked with the consultant to design, implement, and evaluate an intervention plan. Emphasis was on training of personnel by the consultant in order to promote the school's ability to program for target students. Steps in this child-centered process progressed as follows:

- Student referrals were made to the project director.
- Fifteen target students were selected.
- Project personnel met with school personnel to provide project service overview, clarify expectations, and define responsibilities.
- A technical assistance agreement was drawn-up.
- An initial interview was conducted by consultant to determine intervention priorities, gather information, and discuss baseline data collection.
- Baseline data were collected by consultees.
- Functional analysis was conducted by the consultant and consultees.
- A written intervention plan was developed.
- Intervention activities were implemented.
- Evaluation reports were provided by the consultant to the school.

Administrative support and commitment to the students' rights to general education were essential components for the success of this consultation project.

Provision of student support through the consulting model is common. As students with special educational needs have been deinstitutionalized over the past twenty years and have returned to their local schools, general educators have sought the assistance of special educators. Special educators have been considered the experts and general educators have been in need of their expertise. This role continues to be viable in special education programming.

Interagency Consulting

The third example of the consulting model is interagency consulting. With the mandate for schools to provide preschool services and transition-from-school-to-work programs, different human service agencies have had to serve as consultants to each other to meet student needs.

The consulting approach used in rural schools has been based on a county extension agent model (McIntosh and Raymond, 1988). A training program was developed through which general education teachers earned a masters degree in special education and served as consultants to other general education teachers. These teachers served as building-level demonstration agents after receiving training in communication skills, curriculum adaptations, and behavioral interventions.

The consulting model was employed by university collaborators with public school teachers in order to modify the teachers' knowledge and conceptual frameworks (Michelsen, 1991). Working in a professional development school, the university partners served as consultants in helping school teachers implement developmentally appropriate practice with primary-aged children. Rather than providing how-to information, university faculty guided teachers in reflection, experimentation, informal study groups, and restructuring of the literacy development program in primary grades. What resulted from this consulting effort were teachers empowered to collaboratively reflect upon and change their professional thinking and practice.

There is increasing potential use of the consulting model across human service agencies. Infant nursing services, head start programs, mental health counselors, juvenile justice authorities, family social services, rehabilitation counselors, and employment counselors all have become integrally important to effective school programs. As students transition from one level of the educational system to the next, one level of service providers will have to serve as consultants to the next level for the most efficient student transition.

BARRIERS TO AND SUPPORTS
FOR THE CONSULTING MODEL

Barriers to the Consulting Model

A primary barrier to the consulting model of collaboration may be the lack of a theory base. West and Idol (1987) have tried to discover a theoretical basis for consultation with little success. They defined consultation as a ". . . triadic interactive relationship among the consultant, the consultee, and the client" (p. 389). Consultation has the following six characteristics:

- Is a helping, problem-solving process
- Involves a professional help giver and help seeker
- Is voluntary
- Employs shared problem solving
- Addresses a current work problem
- Profits the help seeker

In analyzing consultation processes across human service disciplines (education, psychology, guidance counseling, organizational development, and community psychology) the authors could discern no underlying theory base. They concluded that ". . . the use of consultation as an indirect service model has far outdistanced any theoretical or empirical base" (West and Idol, 1987, p. 404). They suggest that the process of consultation would be strengthened by theory building, basic research, and applied research.

Without a theoretical basis, consultation training can become a barrier to effective consultative practice. In a second article, Idol and West (1987) examined training and practice in special educational consultation. They were able to discover nine general categories of competencies essential for training consultants:

- Consultation theory
- Research on consultation theory, training, and practice
- Personal characteristics
- Interactive communication
- Collaborative problem solving
- Systems change
- Equity issues
- Staff development
- Evaluation of effectiveness

They suggested establishing clearer direction for training educational personnel in consultation. They stated that more appropriate policies are needed at the state level in order for local education agencies to provide effective special educational consultation to general educators. Lacking the requisite theoretical foundation, however, effective training becomes difficult.

Resistance to consultation is a major barrier (Margolis, Fish, and Wepner, 1990; Polsgrove and McNeil, 1989). The sources of resistance may be any of the following:

- Lack of participation in the change process
- Fear of loss
- Miscommunication
- Low tolerance for change
- Fear of the unknown

Resistance may result from defensiveness on the part of the consultee to a consultant's attitude of superiority. It is possible to overcome resistance, however, through supportive measures.

This text attempts to begin addressing the lack of theory by providing a theoretical framework in which to think about collaboration. Defensiveness on the part of the consultee may be precluded by considering the concepts in later chapters such as adult and career developmental levels and employment of situational leadership. Awareness of stages in the change process and training for use of decision making strategies that recognize everyone's opinions may prevent conflict and alleviate resistance to the consulting model.

Supports for the Consulting Model

Personal attributes of the consultant may go a long way in overcoming the barriers to use of the consulting model. The consultant's competence, flexibility, facilitativeness, acceptance, and effective service delivery promote confidence in consultation (Margolis, Fish, and Wepner, 1990; Polsgrove and McNeil, 1989). A consultant should be empathetic, provide verbal reinforcement, use effective confrontation, probe for understanding, and reflect the consultee's statements. Cooperative problem solving and program planning reinforce the voluntary nature of the consultative relationship and grant ownership of the process to the consultee. Adhering to the principles of advising (Little, 1985) protects against defensiveness.

The six principles of advising listed in Figure 4.2 include common language, focus, hard evidence, interaction, predictability, and reciprocity. All of these principles are accounted for by employing clinical observation. Common language refers to positive communication. As discussed in Chapter 3, the importance of active listening, clarifying, and paraphrasing to successful collaboration cannot be over emphasized. Focus to the collaboration can be achieved through a preconference in which the collaborators agree upon the problem definition and a means of data collection. Hard evidence is gained through observing and collecting objective data. Interaction occurs as the observer (consultant) and observee (consultee) analyze and discuss the data during a postconference. Predictability is encompassed

---

Common Language

Focus

Hard Evidence

Interaction

Predictability

Reciprocity

FIGURE 4.2   Six Principles of Advising

From Little, J.W. (1985). "Teachers as Teacher Advisors: The Delicacy of Collegial Leadership." *Educational Leadership* 43(3): 34–46. Reprinted with permission of the Association for Supervision and Curriculum Development. Copyright © 1985 by ASCD. All rights reserved.

in the professional trust and rapport that is built and maintained through the consultative collaboration. Reciprocity refers to the professional equity of the collaborative relationship and the fact that the consultee enters into consulting voluntarily with a right to accept or not accept the expert opinions of the consultant.

Administrative support is essential for promoting successful consulting relationships. Administrators can offer support verbally. They can provide time for consulting through creative scheduling. They can defer to a consultant's opinions and value their suggestions to demonstrate support of consulting as a viable model of collaboration.

APPROPRIATE APPLICATION
OF THE CONSULTING MODEL

Appropriate Use

Each of the programs described not only exemplifies use of a consulting model of collaboration, but also demonstrates viability of the model for promoting both teacher and student development. The consulting model applies wherever there is a person in need of information from a more knowledgeable source. This model of collaboration is appropriate for use by university supervisors with interns in any area. Until the intern has grown enough professionally to demonstrate initiative in determining personal professional goals, the supervisor is a consultant. The consulting model should be employed when students with special educational needs are first introduced to general education and when their educational needs change. The consulting model applies to student transition. School personnel may serve as consultants to post-school professionals as they support students with disabilities in post-school environments.

Step-by-Step Application

Step 1—voluntary nature. For the consulting model to be most effective, its use should be voluntary on the parts of both the consultant and the consultee. In addition to voluntary involvement, the consultant, although the recognized expert, should respect areas in which the consultee may be more knowledgeable and should value the consultee's opinions.

Step 2—homework. Before beginning any consulting relationship, the consultant needs to know his/her audience. They should acquire background knowledge of the system in which they are working and tailor their service to fit system needs, as well as individual consultee needs. Gaining thorough knowledge of the system has been emphasized by Arends and Arends (1977) as important for school psychologists and by Idol et al. (1987) for educational consultants. Arends and Arends suggest building and maintaining a relationship with the system, knowing everything possible about the system, tailoring change efforts to the system, and growing with the system. Similarly, Idol et al. recommend reviewing district material, participating in district meetings, observing classrooms, and disseminating consultation program information.

Step 3—advising. While consulting, the consultant should adhere to the principles of advising in order to maintain a constructive relationship with the consultee.

Step 4—self-evaluation. Finally, the consultant should seek personal performance feedback from the consultee and evaluate the effectiveness of his/her consulting efforts. This step can be partially accomplished through the clinical observation forms described in Chapter 3.

Application of Clinical Observation

Clinical observation can be an invaluable tool in the consulting model. Mentors use this cyclical process in providing technical assistance for performance improvement. Consultants working to support students can use the process with teachers, but the focus of observations would be on student, rather than teacher performance. Consultants from different human service agencies can use the clinical observation cycles to observe and analyze effective and ineffective strategies used with individual students.

Although care must be taken when employing this model not to engender defensiveness on the part of the consultee, the consulting model remains an important collaboration strategy in education and the human services.

SUMMARY

This chapter has described the consulting model of collaboration. This model is defined by expert and novice roles. By definition, the roles are unequal. Examples have been given of the consulting model as it has been employed in mentor teacher programs, in mainstreaming students with disabilities into general education, and in interagency partnerships. Supports for and barriers to the consulting model have been explored. Finally, appropriate use of the model has been discussed.

VIGNETTE REPRISE

Sarah's work for the PWI project exemplified the consulting model of collaboration in all three uses described in this chapter. Sarah served as a mentor for the motel staff. She had the expertise for helping them to learn skills for accommodating Marissa's job-related needs. Sarah was supporting Marissa by providing the necessary consultation to the staff. Finally, she served as an interagency consultant between the school and the motel as Marissa transitioned from an educational environment to the world of work.

PORTFOLIO ACTIVITIES

1. *Personal Application:* Outline a consultation plan as the resource teacher in a secondary setting. Address the following:

   - Initiation of the plan
   - Scheduling consulting
   - Documentation of results
   - Modification of the plan if documentation demonstrates that the plan is ineffective

2. *Professional Reflection:* Read the article listed in the references by Polsgrove and McNeil (1989). Contrast the conceptualization of collaboration models with the models as presented in this book.

3. *Action Research:* Interview a first- and a tenth-year teacher. Compare and contrast their views on a mentor teacher program in terms of the following:

   - Program goal
   - Program process
   - Program evaluation
   - Issues with regard to the selection and compensation plan

REFERENCES

Amatea, E.S. (1990). "Shifting the School's Solution: Using Brief Strategic Intervention in Teacher Consultation." *Special Services in the Schools* 6(1–2): 81–98.

Arends, R.I., and Arends, J.H. (1977). *Systems Change Strategies in Educational Settings.* New York: Human Sciences Press.

Gray, W.A., and Gray, M.M. (1985). "Synthesis of Research on Mentoring Beginning Teachers." *Educational Leadership* 43(3): 37–43.

Hanes, R.C., and Mitchell, K.F. (1985). "Teacher Career Development in Charlotte-Mecklenburg." *Educational Leadership* 43(3): 11–13.

Heron, T.E., and Harris, K.C. (1993). *The Educational Consultant.* Austin, TX: Pro-Ed.

Idol, L. (1993). *Special Educator's Consultation Handbook.* Austin, TX: Pro-Ed.

Idol, L., Paolucci-Whitcomb, P., and Nevin, A. (1987). *Collaborative Consultation.* Austin, TX: Pro-Ed.

Idol, L., and West, J.F. (1987). "Consultation in Special Education: II. Training and Practice." *Journal of Learning Disabilities* 20(8): 474–494.

Irvine, J.J. (1985). "The Master Teacher as Mentor: Role Perceptions of Beginning and Master Teachers." *Education* 106(2): 123–130.

Janney, R.E., and Meyer, L.H. (1990). "A Consultation Model to Support Integrated Educational Services for Students with Severe Disabilities and Challenging Behaviors." *Journal of the Association for Persons with Severe Handicaps* 15(3): 186–199.

Joyce, B., and Showers, B. (1982). "The Coaching of Teaching." *Educational Leadership* 40: 4–8.

Joyce, B., and Showers, B. (1983). *Power in Staff Development through Research on Training.* Alexandria, VA: Association for Supervision and Curriculum Development.

Joyce, B., and Weil, M. (1986). *Models of Teaching,* 3d ed. Englewood Cliffs, NJ: Prentice-Hall, Inc.

Joyce, B., Weil, M., and Showers, B. (1992). *Models of Teaching,* 4th ed. Englewood Cliffs, NJ: Prentice-Hall, Inc.

Little, J.W. (1985). "Teachers as Teacher Advisors: The Delicacy of Collegial Leadership." *Educational Leadership* 43(3): 34–36.

Margolis, H., Fish, M., and Wepner, S.B. (1990). "Overcoming Resistance to Prereferral Classroom Interventions." *Special Services in the Schools* 6(1–2): 167–187.

McIntosh, D.K., and Raymond, G.I. (1988). "A Consultation Model for Rural Schools." *Rural Educator* 9(2): 19–21.

Michelsen, S.S. (December 1991). "The University Collaborator: Empowering Teachers' Thinking." Paper presented at the National Reading Conference, Palm Springs, CA.

Moffett, K.L., St. John, J., and Isken, J.A. (1987). "Training and Coaching Beginning Teachers: An Antidote to Reality Shock." *Educational Leadership* 44(5): 34–36.

Polsgrove, L, and McNeil, M. (1989). "The Consultation Process: Research and Practice." *RASE: Remedial and Special Education* 10(1): 6–13.

Schlechty, P.C. (1985). "Evaluation Procedures in the Charlotte-Mecklenburg Career Ladder Plan." *Educational Leadership* 43(3): 14–19.

Sugai, G.M., and Tindal, G.A. (1993). *Effective School Consultation.* Pacific Grove, CA: Brooks/Cole Publishing Co.

Sweeney, J., and Manatt, D. (1984). "A Team Approach to Supervising the Marginal Teacher." *Educational Leadership* 41(7): 25–27.

Tindal, G., Shinn, M., Walz, L., and Germann, G. (1987). "Mainstream Consultation in Secondary Settings: The Pine County Model." *Journal of Special Education* 21(3): 94–106.

Wagner, L.A. (1985). "Ambiguities and Possibilities in California's Mentor Teacher Program." *Educational Leadership* 43(3): 23–29.

West, J.F., and Idol, L. (1987). "School Consultation: I. An Interdisciplinary Perspective on Theory, Models, and Research." *Journal of Learning Disabilities* 20(7): 388–408.

Wiederholt, J.L., Hammill, D.D., and Brown, V.L. (1983). *The Resource Teacher: A Guide to Effective Practices.* Austin, TX: Pro-Ed.

5

THE COACHING MODEL

Vignette

Sarah found that pay for her weekday job coaching was not enough. She could pay for her efficiency apartment or eat, but she could not do both. In addition, one of the classes that she was taking, SPED 412—Teaching Students with Mental Retardation or Severe Disabilities, required a practicum experience. Sarah and one of her new friends in the graduate program decided to become weekend house parents in a local group home. With the exception of Joe in Blue Spruce, and now Marissa in Plainsview, Sarah had few experiences with children or adults who experienced more intense educational or supported living needs. She welcomed the opportunity to become acquainted with the young adults in a group home setting. She seemed to be continually amazed at the variety of supports available in Plainsview, a city of just under 100,000 inhabitants. She wondered if the group home concept might be applicable in Blue Spruce.

Danny lived in the group home. He was a young man with Down's Syndrome. Danny had many independent living skills. He took care of his own personal hygiene. He helped with meal preparation and clean-up in the group home and even assumed responsibility of lead cook once each week. Danny had a paper route; he delivered newspapers early each morning and during the late hours of the afternoon to his customers. He also collected payment for the papers once a month. Danny's biggest problem both in the group home and on his job was his volatile temper. Never a calm or patient individual, Danny could be obstinate, negative, and extremely irritating to his housemates and house parents. Because changes were problematic for Danny, he was especially irritated by and irritating to weekend house parents. In order to restore equanimity in the group home over the weekends, Sarah, her friend, and the weekday house parents decided to act as peer coaches for each other. They would alternately observe each other and record data on Danny's tantruming, antecedent events, and consequences. They would develop a plan to help Danny gain some control over his behavior and would continue to coach each other through correct implementation of their responsibilities for the plan. Sarah and her friend introduced the weekday house parents to the coaching strategies they had been learning in class.

Chapter Outline

Vignette

Chapter Outline

Chapter Content

> *Definition of the Coaching Model*
> *Examples of the Coaching Model*
>> Coaching for Professional Development
>> Coaching for Performance Appraisal
>> Coaching for Problem Solving
> *Barriers to and Supports for the Coaching Model*
>> Barriers to Coaching
>> Supports for Coaching
> *Appropriate Application of the Coaching Model*
>> Appropriate Use
>> Step-by-Step Application
>> Application of Clinical Observation

Summary

Vignette Reprise

Portfolio Activities

References

DEFINITION OF THE COACHING MODEL

The key concept in a coaching model of collaboration is parity. In contrast to a consulting model where one person is an expert and the other is in need of this expertise, participants using a coaching model recognize their complementary strengths and weaknesses. Through alternately fulfilling the roles of coach or the person being coached, participants in this model assist each other. Joyce and Showers (1982; 1983) may be the pioneers of peer coaching. They have used this model extensively with teachers learning to implement different models of teaching.

EXAMPLES OF THE COACHING MODEL

This section presents examples of the coaching model of collaboration being employed in three ways. The first is coaching as a means toward professional development. Used in this way, professionals work in groups of two or more to coach each other toward achievement of professional development goals. Coaching has also been used for performance appraisal. Peer professionals observe and provide evaluative feedback to each other rather than using the traditional administrative appraisal process. The third example of the coaching model is its use by teachers for problem solving and strategy development with regard to meeting the needs of educationally challenging students. Although the examples given are educational, they can easily be generalized for use by professionals in any area of the human services.

Coaching for Professional Development

An early example of coaching has been described by McFaul and Cooper (1984) as peer clinical supervision. Teachers were trained to implement clinical supervision cycles—preconference, observation and data collection, data analysis, postconference, and observer self-evaluation. In eight cycles, the teachers played the roles of peer supervisor or of supervised teacher. The purpose of the cycles was individual teacher development. It was found that teachers could implement the form of clinical supervision which assumed an atmosphere of collegiality and equality. However, this implementation was not always with the intense, in-depth interaction expected by the authors. The teachers seemed reluctant to breach professional etiquette by asking difficult questions about peer performance. Unwilling to offend their co-workers, they were uncomfortable with the possibility so avoided addressing pedagogical issues in any meaningful way. Peer supervisors were able to reinforce each other but could not manage cognitive dissonance or facilitate its resolution.

Using a similar process, teachers employed peer coaching as an alternative to administrative evaluation (Anastos and Ancowitz, 1987). In addition to the clinical cycle, this group used and analyzed videotapes. Although initially teachers resisted observation, disliked being videotaped, and were reluctant to leave their classrooms, final evaluation of the project proved its success. Teachers were motivated to in-depth examination of their teaching, felt empowered by being "in charge" of the observation process, and felt less isolation through developing trust and respect for peers.

Team coaching combines co-teaching and coaching for staff development purposes (Neubert and Bratton, 1987). Rather than observing, the "coach" team teaches, thus becoming a participant observer. The teacher and team coach cooperatively plan, teach, and evaluate a lesson. The benefits of this example for professional development require that the coach meet the following prerequisites:

- A peer with teaching experience
- Knowledgeable and credible in the teacher's eyes
- Available for the teacher when needed
- Able to balance encouragement with critique

Teaching experience is essential for the peer coach to gain credibility. The coached teacher is more likely to trust a coach who "has been there." For coaches to be effective, they must be accessible. Coaching is needed when the teacher has questions, not several weeks later after issues have been resolved. Balancing critique with encouragement makes the critique palatable. Coached teachers will gain from their coaching interactions if they are able to work with a trusted peer who is available to offer constructive criticism and then support improvement efforts.

Chrisco (1989) validated peer assistance. Members of the English department in a Vermont high school were interested in professional support in the form of guidance and insight rather than evaluation. The teachers began to develop a plan for professional growth in a nonthreatening atmosphere. What initially evolved was a three-stage preconference–observation–postconference process. Teachers working together defined the stages individually. Some summarized observations in writing, while others were satisfied with discussion. As teachers continued to coach each other, the coaching assumed different forms. Teachers taught each other new programs, observed specific parts of lessons, wrote and responded to each other in journals, or engaged in longitudinal studies of each other's classes.

The program has been beneficial to the English teachers in at least the following three ways:

- Re-establishing communication among department members
- Rehearsing lessons through the preconference
- Bringing to the conscious level intuitive teaching practice

Because teaching is such an isolated profession, beginning dialogue among department members had a positive effect on teaching performance. Preconference rehearsal allowed lessons to be polished when presented to students. Recent studies have supported the notion that metacognition is valuable for student learning; metacognition of teaching practice will enable teachers to consciously choose the appropriate teaching strategy rather than relying on instinct. Through coaching, the teachers recognized their professional responsibility for helping each other in continuing professional development.

In Marin County, California, teachers based the teacher advisor project on two premises (Kent, 1985):

- Teachers can define their own professional development.
- Assistance on-site is essential to impacting classroom performance.

Participants in the project assumed the roles of teacher advisor or of peer facilitator. Teacher advisor and peer facilitator positions were similar but had different areas of responsibility. The teacher advisor worked with staff members at two or three schools and was responsible for training and facilitation. The peer facilitator coordinated a network or worked with one school staff member but was involved in limited training or facilitating.

In either role, responsibilities fell into the areas of resource linker, facilitator, trainer, colleague coach, or supervisor. The resource linker found or developed materials, located speakers, planned field trips, or linked teachers. Facilitating involved assisting a group of teachers in their collaborative efforts. A facilitator might lead a group through the process of consensus building on any educationally related issue. Trainers established common technical language and trained for instructional skills, cooperative learning strategies, peer observation techniques, and classroom management. Coaches followed training with intensive in-class practice. The role of supervisor was rare. It demanded respect and trust among the site administrator, teacher advisor or peer facilitator, and teacher. As a supervisor, neither teacher advisors nor peer facilitators evaluated teaching performance.

Professional growth was supported through peer coaching in a Sonoma County, California school district (Raney and Robbins, 1989). A peer coaching program was implemented to help newly hired teachers. Participants in this program went through extensive training sessions for their coaching role. Training included examples of peer coaching, observation instruments for coaching, factors influencing peer relationships, conferencing skills, communication skills, and change theory. Observation and conferencing were based on the clinical observation process. In fact, much of the training information mirrors topics of this text. Figure 5.1 outlines specific content of the training that coaches received for this project. One benefit of the program was the permission given to teachers for experimentation. No longer did teachers feel that they had to be perfect. As a staff, they began to focus on continuing development in instruction and classroom management.

Session 1	*Overview of research on peer coaching* *Context for peer coaching*

- Collaborative goal structures in schools
- Peer coaching, school norms, and culture
- Social and technical principles of coaching
- Organizing for peer coaching
- Exemplary peer coaching models

Sessions 2 & 3	*Overview of observation instruments for coaching*

- Interaction analysis
- Time-off-task
- Drop-in observation
- Cognitive coaching
- Script-taping
- Checklists

Session 4	*Factors influencing peer coaching relationships* *Model of factors influencing teacher thinking and behavior*

- Modality preferences
- Educational beliefs
- Cognitive style

Session 5	*Advanced conferencing skills*

- Preconferencing
- Observing
- Postconferencing

Session 6	*Fine-tuning communication skills*

- Mediational questions
- Probing for specificity
- Identifying and staying aware of presuppositions

Session 7	*Change theory and effective staff development practices*

- What the research says
- Implications for peer coaching
- Planning for maintenance

FIGURE 5.1 Peer Coaching Training Sessions

From Raney, P., and Robbins, P. (1989). "Professional Growth and Support through Peer Coaching." *Educational Leadership* 46(8): 35–38. Reprinted with permission of the Association for Supervision and Curriculum Development. Copyright © 1989 by ASCD. All rights reserved.

Similar benefits have been reported by the Ann Arbor public schools as a result of peer coaching (Sparks and Bruder, 1987). Teachers in two schools videotaped teaching episodes before beginning peer coaching, attended brief training in observation strategies and giving feedback, and selected coaching partners. Participants had the help of a consultant to discuss coaching and to develop new coaching skill areas throughout the project. As a result of peer coaching, teachers received frequent feedback on their teaching, increased collegiality, felt freer to experiment with new teaching techniques, and allayed concerns with peer observation.

Costa and Kallick (1993) describe coaching as a critical friend relationship. The critical friend is a trusted peer who asks clarifying questions, provides data, and offers a constructive critique. The critical friend serves as a mirror of performance, allowing the learner to view self through the perspective of another. The process of critical friendship involves several steps:

- The learner describes a practice and requests feedback.
- The critical friend asks questions for understanding and clarifying the practice.
- The learner sets goals.
- The critical friend provides feedback, raises questions, and critiques the learner's practice.
- Both learner and critical friend reflect in writing on the process.

As in any coaching situation, the purpose of the critical friend relationship is supported, professional development.

If peers have the luxury of time to develop the rapport and trust necessary for honest, in-depth dialogue, peer coaching can support teachers' efforts toward critical self-analysis and ongoing personal professional improvement. Hawkey (1995) has suggested peer coaching between student teachers as a way to develop technical skills and promote reflective practice. Peer coaches do not appear as intimidating to student teachers as do university supervisors or even mentor teachers. Using clinical observation for analyzing microteaching episodes enhanced pre-service students' pedagogical skill development. Similarly, in-service teachers can exploit the support of a peer coach without the anxiety produced by administrative evaluation.

Coaching for Performance Appraisal

A second way in which the coaching model has been employed is in performance appraisal. Peer evaluation has had the advantage of being an ongoing process, rather than the traditional once a year administrative observation. Because peers become accustomed to being observed and having additional adults in the classroom, the anxiety produced by infrequent supervisory visits is allayed. The process can facilitate teacher development in a more constructive process than traditional appraisal.

Teachers in an elementary school in Colorado with the support of their school administration developed a peer appraisal process (Walen and DeRose, 1993). The new process took several years to implement fully. During the planning year, teachers met socially in order to build rapport and trust. They discussed goals for the new process. During the second year, five teachers volunteered for peer appraisals. Working in appraisal pairs to observe and provide written feedback to a third teacher provided an additional way to collaborate. The teachers employed a before- and after-school discussion group, rather than individual conferences, in order to increase the sense of support. Teachers discovered that as individuals they learned more from observing their peers' performance than from being observed and critiqued.

Team supervision was also used in Pittsburgh's school improvement program (SIP) (Bickel and Artz, 1984). Working as teams, instructional supervisors and principals coached teachers. As opposed to traditional supervision that involved short-term crisis planning, fragmented service delivery, isolation from colleagues, separation of general and special education, and a dichotomous supervisor–principal relationship, the team supervision offered teachers the following:

- Data-based instructional planning
- Focused attention and time
- Team planning and working
- General-special education collaboration
- Supervisor–principal collaboration

Team supervision promoted instructional improvement through the use of objective data and changed the supervisory role from administrative to supportive. The SIP program allowed supervisors to be perceived as coaches rather than evaluators.

Similarly, a California school developed professional partnerships as part of the evaluation process (Stobbe, 1993). Teachers were grouped into teams of six teachers who observed each other's classrooms on a monthly basis. Working in dyads, teachers met with the principal and a facilitator at the beginning of the school year to define goals. Partners met before an observation to define lesson focus and after the observation to discuss results. During quarterly meetings with the principal and facilitator, participants monitored progress and set future direction. Through the professional partnership, information was gathered to assist individual teachers in better understanding the instructional dynamics of their classes. Professional development was enhanced through improved observation and communication skills as well as teachers' increasing ability to conduct action research with regard to their teaching. The school administration became more involved in instructional issues. Finally, the professional partnerships project opened classroom doors and decreased participants' experience of educational isolation.

South Carolina's Program for Effective Teaching (PET) used coaching to evaluate application of in-service teacher training (Mandeville and Rivers, 1989). Coaching was defined as formative observations and conferences directed toward implementation of a Hunter-based instructional model. Coaching included classroom observation and note taking, analysis, and pre- and post-observation conferences. Teachers responded positively to both the Hunter-based instructional training and to peer coaching. PET program evaluation suggested that coaches required extensive training themselves to be optimally effective, and that common terminology, collegial cooperation, and long-term commitment were essential components of a coaching model.

Through contract negotiation in a New York school district, teachers were able to change traditional evaluation procedures to a more collegial approach (Black, 1993). Principals began to see themselves as coaches rather than as appraisers and took their role as instructional leaders seriously. In contrast to unannounced evaluation walkthroughs, principals shared appraisal forms with teachers, held preobservation conferences, scripted lessons, remained for an entire class, and shared data analysis with teachers. Principals were able to promote a win-win evaluative atmosphere and teachers were able to grow professionally with administrative coaching.

An Illinois principal rebelled against the traditional appraisal system and proposed coaching to her staff as an alternative (Rooney, 1993). Need for change in evaluation procedures came with the realization that the following assumptions were untenable:

- The principal had the power to change teacher behavior.
- Teachers were "broken" and needed to be "fixed."
- Although only a minority of teachers were incompetent, a remediation plan should be developed for everyone.
- Ranking teachers as "excellent," "satisfactory," or "unsatisfactory" led to instructional improvement.

Instead, teachers and principal agreed the teachers would visit one another for observation purposes while the principal substituted in one or the other's classroom. Teachers would meet to plan their visits and to dialogue after an observation. As a result of the new procedures, barriers between teachers broke down, peer coaching became the school norm, individual teacher differences were respected, post-observation discussions evolved into co-teaching, continued support, and ongoing professional encouragement. Teachers became responsible for their own and each other's growth.

If schools could come to be learning environments for faculty and staff, as well as students, then peer appraisals would be the norm. Professionals do not require "supervision" because they strive for excellent performance and welcome supportive performance evaluations. True professionals welcome peer reviews and thrive on the professional growth that they engender.

Coaching for Problem Solving

Johnson, Pugach, and Cook (1993; Pugach and Johnson, 1989) described a different form of peer coaching. They have used a peer collaboration problem-solving model to facilitate general education classroom intervention strategies for at-risk students. The problem initiator and solution facilitator work through four steps—problem description, problem clarification, strategy brainstorming, and strategy evaluation as illustrated in Figure 5.2. Teacher dyads have been trained to fill both roles. The initiator is the owner of a problem and seeks the facilitator to assist with finding a problem solution. The facilitator paraphrases the problem as described by the initiator and asks clarifying questions for a true understanding of the problem situation. Together they brainstorm possible strategies for addressing the problem, but the initiator retains ownership by judging the potential of each suggestion and choosing the strategy to implement. Both initiator and facilitator

---

1. Problem Description and Clarifying Questions
2. Problem Summary
3. Outcome Prediction for Limited Interventions
4. Impementation Plan and Evaluation Strategy

FIGURE 5.2   Pugach and Johnson Peer Collaboration Model Initiator/Facilitator Process

From Johnson, L.J., Pugach, M.C., and Cook, R. (1993). "Peer Collaboration as a Means to Facilitate Collegial Support to Reduce Teacher Isolation and Facilitate Classroom Problem Solving in Rural Areas." *RSEQ* 12(2): 21–26. Reprinted with permission.

develop an evaluation plan and agree to a subsequent meeting time for determining plan effectiveness. Although proposed as a prereferral process before formal referral to special education, this peer-assistance process can be applied to a wide variety of situations.

BARRIERS TO AND SUPPORTS
FOR THE COACHING MODEL

Barriers to Coaching

Barriers to the coaching model include the traditional organizational structure of schools and most human services institutions, as well as common misperceptions of professional etiquette. Bureaucratic organizations are based on a hierarchical structure with a definite chain-of-command and specified roles and responsibilities. The coaching model involves changing that structure to incorporate responsibility sharing and role reciprocity.

In addition, traditional perceptions of professional etiquette including the fierce individualism of teaching, insecurity with the appropriate pedagogy for another's discipline, and unwillingness to grapple with difficult issues may present obstacles to coaching (Little, 1985; McFaul and Cooper, 1984; Walen and DeRose, 1993).

Supports for Coaching

First and foremost, for the coaching model to be successful, the peers involved must have developed professional rapport and trust (Costa and Kallick, 1993; Krajewski, 1984; Little, 1985; McFaul and Cooper, 1984). Costa and Kallick (1993) list prerequisites for successful critical friendships:

- The nature of the relationship should not be judgmental or evaluative.
- Active listening, idea clarification, and encouragement of specificity are essential.
- Value judgments should be offered only upon request.
- Integrity of response to the learner's work is important.
- Advocacy for the learner's success.

These prerequisites parallel the principles of advising advocated by Little (1985). (See Chapter 4, Figure 4.2.)

Administrators can support the coaching model by providing time for peer coaches to meet, by employing or acting as substitutes in peer teachers' rooms while they observe one another, and by recognizing the value of coaching data for documenting professional growth.

APPROPRIATE APPLICATION
OF THE COACHING MODEL

Appropriate Use

The peer coaching model has application beyond educational settings. Peer professionals in any of the human services can coach each other through professional development or client-centered service issues. Coaching applies to immediate problem solution, as well as to professional growth in either formative or evaluative environments. Coaching involves two or more professionals trading the reciprocal roles of critic and performer for the purpose of supporting and encouraging each other's continuing professional development.

Step-by-Step Application

Step 1—exposure. For teachers to be comfortable with coaching, the process should be introduced at the pre-service level. During their undergraduate training, student teachers can be videotaped and coached by peers as they develop pedagogical skills. At Montana State University—Billings, students enroll in sophomore, junior, and senior level field experiences. At each level, video taping lessons is encouraged. Students support each other in seminars throughout each field experience semester. The next step is exposure to and practice with peer clinical observation, either in-class or using the videos, followed by peer debriefing and professional dialogue.

Step 2—formation of coaching dyads. Initial pairing of teachers for coaching experiences cannot be arbitrary. Coaching participants should be compatible in pedagogical philosophies, at least at the beginning. As teachers gain experience and confidence with this form of collaboration, pairing teachers whose work is based on different foundations can be a mind-expanding experience for both individuals. Initial experience with this model by two people who are not personally and professionally compatible, however, is disastrous.

Step 3—administrative restructuring. Educational institutions require modifications in professional role expectations, as well as in scheduling for implementation of the coaching model. Administrators and teachers will have to abandon the fierce pride in individual ownership of a particular class or group of students. Administrators will have to encourage teachers to open their doors to each other, and teachers will have to accept the vulnerability that accompanies peer visitation. In addition, administrators and faculty will have to develop schedules that permit blocks of time for intense peer interaction.

Step 4—paired professional reflection. Unlike the consulting model that calls for consultant self-evaluation, the coaching model requires professional reflection by the coaching pairs. The clinical observation process evaluation forms suggested in Chapter 3 can be applied to this reflective process. They should be completed in a dialogue format by both the coach and performer, however, rather than on an individual basis.

Application of Clinical Observation

Clinical observation has been an essential tool for the coaching model. Peer coaching requires observation of instruction and appropriate conferencing in order for the peer coach to support growth. Peer appraisals cannot happen without the use of the clinical observation process. When coaching for problem solving, as with consulting for student support, coaches use clinical observation with the focus on students rather than on the peer professional.

SUMMARY

This chapter has defined the coaching model of collaboration. Parity and reciprocity are the hallmarks of coaching. Examples of coaching for professional development, performance appraisal, and problem solving have been discussed. Finally, appropriate application of successful coaching and supports as well as barriers to the model have been delineated.

VIGNETTE REPRISE

Coaching was an amazing means of support for all involved with Danny. Sarah and her friend who shared weekend group home duties, and the weekday houseparents, knowing that they had each others' support, were able to cope with Danny's temper. Both teams found that they needed time to meet with each other on a regular basis. Time was needed for observations of their different styles in dealing with Danny. Time was needed to debrief on successful and unsuccessful interactions. Not only did a strong sense of mutual support grow between the coaching teams, but support for Danny grew from the process as well.

PORTFOLIO ACTIVITIES

1. *Personal Application:* Choose a teaching peer with whom you have established a good working relationship. Each of you choose a student who is experiencing difficulty either academically or behaviorally. Work through the four steps of the Pugach and Johnson (1989) model as initiator of your own student problem and as facilitator of your peer's student problem.

2. *Professional Reflection:* Read the McFaul and Cooper (1984) article describing a peer clinical supervision study. Read the responses to their article by Goldsberry (1984) and by Krajewski (1984) in the same issue of *Educational Leadership.* What do you think?

3. *Action Research:* Work with a school administrator whom you know to initiate a teacher appraisal process involving coaching. You might try the following protocol:

- Establish two appraisal strands. One would involve the traditional administrator visit in order to observe and to complete the requisite checklist. The other would involve dyads of teachers working together to establish personal professional goals, then coaching each other in order to reach those goals.
- These two strands might be implemented throughout the school with every teacher experiencing both. They could be implemented as parallel strands with half of the teachers on one track and half on the other.
- Have teachers compare their thoughts about the two processes before beginning the project, about mid-year, and at the end of school. Suggest avenues for further study.

REFERENCES

Anastos, J., and Ancowitz, R. (1987). "A Teacher-Directed Peer Coaching Project." *Educational Leadership* 45(3): 40–42.

Bickel, W.E., and Artz, N.J. (1984). "Improving Instruction through Focused Team Supervision." *Educational Leadership* 41(7): 22–23.

Black, S. (1993). "How Teachers Are Reshaping Evaluation Procedures." *Educational Leadership* 51(2): 38–42.

Chrisco, I.M. (1989). "Peer Assistance Works." *Educational Leadership* 46(8): 31–32.

Costa, A.L., and Kallick, B. (1993). "Through the Lens of a Critical Friend." *Educational Leadership* 51(2): 49–51.

Goldsberry, L.F. (1984). "Reality—Really?" *Educational Leadership* 41(7): 10–11.

Hawkey, K. (1995). "Learning from Peers: The Experience of Student Teachers in School-Based Teacher Education." *Journal of Teacher Education* 46(3): 175–183.

Johnson, L.J., Pugach, M.C., and Cook, R. (1993). "Peer Collaboration as a Means to Facilitate Collegial Support to Reduce Teacher Isolation and Facilitate Classroom Problem Solving in Rural Areas." *Rural Special Education Quarterly* 12(2): 21–26.

Joyce, B., and Showers, B. (1982). "The Coaching of Teaching." *Educational Leadership* 40: 4–8.

Joyce, B., and Showers, B. (1983). *Power in Staff Development through Research on Training.* Alexandria, VA: Association for Supervision and Curriculum Development.

Kent, K.M. (1985). "A Successful Program of Teachers Assisting Teachers." *Educational Leadership* 43(3): 30–33.

Krajewski, R.J. (1984). "No Wonder It Didn't Work!" *Educational Leadership* 41(7): 11.

Little, J.W. (1985). "Teachers as Teacher Advisors: The Delicacy of Collegial Leadership." *Educational Leadership* 43(3): 34–36.

Mandeville, G.K., and Rivers, J. (1989). "Is the Hunter Model a Recipe for Supervision?" *Educational Leadership* 46(8): 39–43.

McFaul, S.A., and Cooper, J.M. (1984). "Peer Clinical Supervision: Theory vs. Reality." *Educational Leadership* 41(7): 4–9.

Neubert, G.A., and Bratton, E.C. (1987). "Team Coaching: Staff Development Side by Side." *Educational Leadership* 44(5): 29–32.

Pugach, M.C., and Johnson, L.J. (1989). "Prereferral Interventions: Progress, Problems and Challenges." *Exceptional Children* 56(3): 217–226.

Raney, P., and Robbins, P. (1989). "Professional Growth and Support through Peer Coaching." *Educational Leadership* 46(8): 35–38.

Rooney, J. (1993). "Teacher Evaluation: No More 'Super' Vision." *Educational Leadership* 51(2): 43–44.

Sparks, G.M., and Bruder, S. (1987). "Before and After Peer Coaching." *Educational Leadership* 45(3): 54–57.

Stobbe, C. (1993). "Professional Partnerships." *Educational Leadership* 51(2): 40–41.

Walen, E., and DeRose, M. (1993). "The Power of Peer Appraisals." *Educational Leadership* 51(2): 45–48.

6

THE TEAMING MODEL

Vignette

One evening in Sarah's graduate collaboration class, a Mexican-American woman made a presentation telling about her son, Nick, in Texas. Nick was a young person with moderate mental retardation and autism. Although he lived in his own apartment and had a position as a bus person in a local restaurant, Nick required daily support. His father had recently changed employment, and Nick's immediate family had moved from one of the metropolitan areas in Texas to Plainsview. Nick wanted to remain in the familiarity of the barrio. In order to support Nick in his efforts to live independently, a group of close family friends volunteered to be "Friends-of-Nick." They shared responsibility for checking with Nick daily, reminding him about his medication, and assisting him with meal planning and grocery shopping, keeping doctor, dentist and counseling appointments, and maintaining workplace responsibilities. Each member took the lead in a different aspect of support for Nick. The team members met regularly to discuss any pertinent problems or needs. They shared decision making both with Nick and among themselves. Without this collaborative teaming, Nick would have had to move with his family to a considerably smaller city with a culture foreign to him and lacking any familiar faces save those of his family. In addition, Nick's limited English proficiency would have made finding even menial labor quite difficult in Plainsview. Sarah knew without a doubt that such teaming could be just the vehicle needed to support her students with less severe disabilities as they left the safety of a near reservation school to seek employment in Blue Spruce or other small towns on the high line.

Chapter Outline

Vignette

Chapter Outline

Chapter Content

> *Definition of the Teaming Model*
> *Examples of the Teaming Model*
>> Teaming as Co-Teaching
>> Teaming as Support for Professional Development
>> Teaming for Problem Solving
> *Barriers to and Supports for the Teaming Model*
>> Barriers to Teaming
>> Supports for Teaming
> *Appropriate Application of the Teaming Model*
>> Appropriate Use
>> Step-by-Step Application
>> Application of Clinical Observation

Summary

Vignette Reprise

Portfolio Activities

References

DEFINITION OF THE TEAMING MODEL

The teaming model of collaboration is completely interactive. Unlike the consulting model in which one person is an expert, participants in an interactive team take the lead role as situations dictate. Also, unlike the coaching model, where participants take turns owning or assisting with a problem, members of an interactive team share ownership of the purpose and outcomes of their collaborative efforts. Morsink, Thomas, and Correa (1991) have described this type of collaboration in their text, *Interactive Teaming,* as do Idol, Nevin, and Paolucci-Whitcomb (1994) in the second edition of *Collaborative Consultation.*

EXAMPLES OF THE TEAMING MODEL

Examples of the teaming model of collaboration discussed in this section fall into three more specific subcategories—examples of co-teaching, examples of team support, and examples of team problem solving. Co-teaching is defined as the teaming of two or more teachers as instructors for a group of students, a specific course, or an individual class. Team support refers to teams of teachers assisting each other with development toward individual professional goals. The examples of team problem solving are in reference to the prereferral or special education IEP processes. While the examples of teaming are all educational, they can easily be generalized across the human services professions.

Teaming as Co-Teaching

Friend and Cook (1994) have described six different formats for co-teaching. In the first, one person teaches while the other observes both the teaching and the students. The second places one teacher as the primary instructor and the other as a "drifter" who provides assistance to students throughout the lesson. The third format involves both instructors as teachers on a parallel basis, that is, two lessons are occurring simultaneously. The fourth approach to co-teaching is station teaching in which teachers exchange groups of students and repeat instruction for each group at different times. Alternative teaching, the fifth format, involves one teacher providing remedial instruction to a group of students while the other teacher provides enrichment activities for another student group. Finally, team teaching involves both teachers delivering the same instruction at the same time.

These different forms of co-teaching are useful for different purposes and involve more or less intensive co-planning by the co-teachers. The first approach involving one person as teacher and one as observer requires little co-planning. It is used in new co-teaching situations or to answer questions about students. Minimal joint planning is needed for the second approach as well. Here one person teaches while the other assists students. Parallel teaching requires a medium amount of collaborative planning. It is a good strategy to use when there is need for a smaller student-to-teacher ratio. Likewise, station teaching requires a medium amount of joint planning. Station teaching can be used for review, to teach several topics simultaneously, or for delivering content that is not hierarchical. Alternative teaching is appropriate when some students require remediation, but others are ready for enrichment activities. Because each teacher is teaching to different objectives, although on the same topic, a medium amount of co-planning is necessary. Finally, team teaching requiring a high degree of collaborative planning is useful for demonstrating cooperative interaction for students to model, and for teaching a complex topic requiring expertise of both individual instructors.

A program of co-teaching between general and special educators has been described by Redditt (1991). In order to facilitate the integration of students with special educational needs into general education class-rooms, teachers paired in general-special education teacher teams. Cooperative teaching demanded commitment, flexibility, and time for planning, but resulted in fewer at-risk students, a decline in the number of special education referrals, decreased stigmatization of students with disabilities, and modeling of collaboration by teachers for students. Teachers were able to view their classrooms from different perspectives.

Several steps were suggested as implementation strategies for developing a co-teaching program:

- Provide information about multidisciplinary collaboration to school faculty
- Educate faculty about the benefits of general–special education collaboration and integration
- Seek administrative incentives for general and special educators who are willing to collaborate
- Allow teachers the option of whether or not to co-teach
- Gain administrative support in the form of scheduling for co-planning time, preventing interruption of co-teaching episodes for crisis intervention, and promoting positive public relations about co-practice
- Collect evaluation data on students and teachers before beginning the process
- Develop a school-wide multidisciplinary team to set goals for co-teaching
- Train school personnel in collaborative strategies
- Involve parents in the co-teaching program development
- Plan for formative and summative evaluation of co-teaching

Before implementation of any new educational routine, provision of basic information about the change is important. Allowing the innovation to be on a voluntary basis and including both school and community stakeholders in decision making and planning gives everyone involved ownership. Establishing participant ownership precludes sabotage of change efforts by individuals who feel that co-teaching has been administratively dictated to them. Intensive training before trying new teaching methods allays participant anxiety with regard to personal performance. Ongoing evaluation will demonstrate where adjustments are needed in co-teaching and will provide objective data for making informed decisions about practice. These suggestions will be repeated in Chapter 9 as strategies for preventing unnecessary conflict among teachers as collaborative practice becomes the educational norm.

Co-teaching necessitates personnel training. In order for teachers to model for students the social and communication skills needed for cooperative teaching and learning, they must be taught themselves

(Sharan and Sharan, 1987). The experiential learning model (ELM) was developed for training adults cooperative learning theory and strategy. The ELM workshop was implemented in the following four stages:

- Stage 1—Concrete experience with examples of cooperative learning
- Stage 2—Observations and reflections on the concrete experiences
- Stage 3—Formation of abstract concepts and generalizations in order to define a common professional vocabulary with regard to cooperative learning
- Stage 4—Testing applications of cooperative learning concepts in new situations

Training teachers in a variety of cooperative learning strategies allows them to apply cooperative learning to co-teaching and to analyze their co-teaching efforts.

Co-teaching was extended across organizational boundaries by a Ford Foundation project aimed at alleviating the professional isolation of mathematics teachers (Nelson, 1986). Several cities developed mathematics collaboratives linking groups of mathematics professionals from high schools, institutions of higher education (IHE), and private industry. By lessening teacher isolation and increasing intellectual stimulation through links with the greater mathematics community, the project improved mathematics education.

The project took different forms in different cities. In Los Angeles, mathematics departments in three high schools joined with businesses and IHE's for program development and community resource identification. In Cleveland, high school mathematics teachers served as interns in industry and industrial retraining centers in order to experience industrial needs and to be able to change their high school curricula accordingly. In Minneapolis/St. Paul, teachers participated with industrial mathematicians and university faculty in seminars addressing complex mathematics problems. Regular meetings to discuss interesting mathematics topics rejuvenated the teachers' interest in math and confidence in themselves as theoretical mathematicians. In San Francisco, teachers worked with physicists on mathematical models explaining physical systems and subsequently jointly planned math and physics projects. Collaborative teaming beyond traditional educational boundaries renewed teachers' enthusiasm for their discipline, increased receptivity to new ideas, promoted resourcefulness, and rejuvenated teachers' encouragement of student effort.

Gallivan-Fenlon (1994) has described the use of a transdisciplinary team in a preschool setting. Preschool services for children with disabilities must be integrated across service providers in order to optimize service delivery to children. The transdisciplinary team was characterized by information sharing across traditional disciplinary boundaries. Therapists, related service providers and teachers taught each other skills and techniques useful across settings. Such sharing of expertise unified services into a more coherently articulated whole. The team developed individual family service plans (IFSP) and provided integrated therapy throughout the child's life space. Provision of service in a natural setting prevented splinter skill development, lack of generalization, and disruption of a normalized schedule. This example of the teaming model of collaboration applied team service delivery across human service agencies to meet individual student needs.

Teaming as Support for Professional Development

Collegial support groups exemplify a different purpose for teaming (Paquette, 1987). Teachers in a Canadian high school developed teams that met regularly to support the members' professional growth activities. Through a three-phase process, participants achieved personal professional goals. Phase one involved team building activities. During phase two, group members met monthly for three hours to learn a new concept and plan personal applications. Phase three was a summary session for sharing successes.

Team supervision has a similar purpose, that of instructional improvement (Bickel and Artz, 1984). The supervisory team, consisting of a project director, a teacher, one special education supervisor, and two general education supervisors, was part of Pittsburgh's school improvement program (SIP). The SIP supervisory process was discussed in Chapter 5 as an example of coaching, but the SIP supervisors exemplify teaming. Members of the team interacted as individuals sharing ownership of school improvement goals. As a team, they coached school personnel toward goal achievement.

Similarly, the team supervision process, described in Chapter 4 (Sweeny and Manatt, 1984), is an example of a team working as consultants. A team of teachers served as advisors to marginal teachers who did not demonstrate instructional competence. The advisors teamed with administrators to determine the areas in need of improvement for individual teachers. Administrators then teamed to decide whether to discontinue advising, to continue advising, or to move for dismissal. The process between the teacher and the team was in the consulting model, but the process among advising and administrative team members exemplifies the teaming model of collaboration.

The Learning Exchange, a nonprofit resource center in Kansas City, was developed to broaden the team supervision concept to include local businesses and foundations, as well as area educators (Bradford, 1986). A cadre of teachers and administrators was selected from area applicants.

Cadre members attended monthly study group meetings and participated in forty hours of workshops after initial training in adult learning theory and effective instruction. Each participating school district donated twenty released days for each cadre member, thus providing a service pool of professionals available for in-service workshops, college credit classes, and peer coaching. With this broadened approach, area schools had more access to better staff development resources, and development of in-house expertise ensured lasting, long-term benefit.

Professional development support teams (PDST) have been used in the Santa Cruz City Schools, California, in lieu of traditional evaluation (Krovetz and Cohick, 1993). Teachers participating in PDST's determined areas for professional development. At the high school, teachers investigated performance-based assessment, developed a career paths model, explored the use of cooperative learning, and developed writing prompts. Junior high school teachers revised the seventh grade curriculum to include integrated thematic units and performance-based evaluation. Elementary school participants planned and taught a multi-aged primary grade program. Faculty on all three sites began discourse about practice, observed each other teaching, planned cooperatively, and designed, evaluated, and revised curricula. The PDST project allowed site faculty to individualize staff development efforts. As a result, teachers improved the quality of their work, built professional relationships, and developed shared professional goals.

Donaldson (1993) has described collaborative school change as "working smarter together" (p. 12). He defined the five stage cycle of progress as:

- Criticism
- Self-examination
- Goal setting
- New efforts
- Consolidation

Administrators and teachers redefined their roles to share responsibility for seeking creative solutions, accept responsibility for the institution, and participate in crucial school decisions. Collaborative teaming established new working relationships through which the administration treated school faculty as a responsible community of adults capable of setting goals and managing resources.

Benefits of professional cooperative efforts have been demonstrated by the research of Johnson and Johnson (1987). Social interdependence can be structured competitively, individualistically, or cooperatively. A competitive structure maximizes personal gain at the expense of colleagues. An individualistic structure promotes individual goals unrelated to co-professionals or the institution as a whole. In a cooperative structure, peers work together to achieve outcomes benefiting each other and success is jointly determined. A meta-analysis of research demonstrated that cooperation promoted higher achievement, greater social support, and higher individual self-esteem.

Teaming for Problem Solving

A third way in which the teaming model of collaboration has been used is for team problem solving. Often employed to determine pre-special education referral strategies, team problem solving has also been employed for individual student programming and placement decisions, or for decisions addressing school-wide issues.

Prereferral intervention before formal referral for special education evaluation can result in decreasing the number of inappropriate special education referrals and in successfully maintaining at-risk youngsters in general education programs. Traditional prereferral intervention has been in the form of consulting, but a teaming approach may be more effective. Prereferral teaming is based on several underlying assumptions (Pugach and Johnson, 1989):

- Assumption 1—Prereferral is a function of general education
- Assumption 2—Teaming is a multidirectional activity
- Assumption 3—Classroom teachers have the expertise to solve many classroom problems
- Assumption 4—All problems do not require the same team members in order to develop solutions

Graden (1989) concurs that for prereferral intervention efforts to be optimally effective, they should be based on collaboration maintaining responsibility with general education teachers and employing systematic problem-solving approaches.

Calling teaming "collaborative consultation," West and Idol (1990) defined it as ". . . an interactive process which enables people with diverse expertise to generate creative solutions to mutually defined problems" (p. 23). They suggested six stages for purposeful and efficient problem solving:

- Stage 1—Goal/entry
- Stage 2—Problem identification
- Stage 3—Intervention recommendations
- Stage 4—Implementation recommendations
- Stage 5—Evaluation
- Stage 6—Redesign

This six-stage teaming process has been used by teacher assistance teams, intervention assistance teams, school-based resource teams, student support teams, and child study teams.

Each stage in the process is essential for efficient and effective team functioning. Group consensus with regard to the team goals and mutual understanding of the problem is necessary for maintaining team focus. Group determination of possible interventions and group agreement on the implementation plan will assure that each team member is consistent in plan application. Joint evaluation and redesign of efforts as needed will maintain the ongoing problem solving nature of quality group interaction.

A collaborative decision-making model based on five options was developed for selecting the least intrusive intervention strategy appropriate for individual students (Donaldson and Christiansen, 1990). Options included behavior management, part-time assistance, instructional options, instructional options combined with part-time assistance, or full-time assistance. These options were considered consistent with the mandate for provision of a continuum of services in special education law.

Contained in the two phases of the model, entry and instruction/resource analysis, were several decision points. During the entry phase, team members determined times during the school day when the student experienced learning problems. During the instruction and resource analysis phase, teams members evaluated variables affecting student success in general education. They determined if part-time, in-class assistance would be effective. The team next decided if instructional modifications were warranted. Finally, the team determined whether or not full-time, in-class assistance would be beneficial for the student, and, if not, team members considered pull-out services. This model was reversed for use as a tool for exiting students from special educational services.

Another example of team problem solving is the collaborative options—outcome planner (COOP) (Welch, Judge, Anderson, Bray, Child, and Franke, 1990). The COOP process involves four steps and answers thirteen questions. The first step for implementing COOP is gaining administrative support and planning a workshop. The workshop, step two, defines and demonstrates the prereferral process with simulated practice by groups of teachers. Step three requires designation of a location for filing completed COOPs. Finally, the process is subjected to continual evaluation and refinement by those involved. Questions to be answered included:

- How can the situation or behavior be described?
- What has been tried to resolve the situation?
- Where and when does the situation occur?
- What is an area of individual strength?

- What appears to motivate the individual?
- What others are involved?
- What are options for intervention?
- Which options hold the most potential for success?
- What is the chosen behavioral objective?
- What are evaluation criteria?
- How and when will progress be measured?
- What are the responsibilities of team members for the plan?
- When is the next meeting scheduled?

Although written to make decisions about student programming, the questions could be easily modified for addressing institutional decision making, as well.

A final team decision-making process to be presented is the McGill action planning system, also know as making action plans (MAPS) (Forest and Lusthaus, 1990; Forest and Pearpoint, 1992; Vandercook, York, and Forest, 1989). MAPS has been employed in the IEP process in order to focus educational decision making on the individual, rather than on the individual's disability category. The MAPS process is a means of including peers and parents in special educational planning and exemplifies the teaming model of collaboration. The MAPS system asks questions of the child and other significant people in his/her life in order to plan the most supportive educational program possible. The eight essential questions include: (1) What is a MAP? (2) What is the story? (3) What is your dream? (4) What is your nightmare? (5) Who are you? (6) What are your unique gifts? (7) What are your needs? (8) What is the plan of action to avoid the nightmare and to make the dream come true? Each member of the MAPS team has an opportunity to answer the questions posed about the student. Each member's contributions are equally valued.

To complete a MAP, any person interested in the outcome should be invited to participate. MAPS participants come together in a comfortable setting with the understanding that no one participant is any more important or has any more to contribute than the others. Chart paper and colorful markers should be available for recording each participant's answer to each of the eight MAPS questions. A facilitator maintains focus and momentum during the process, summarizes the group's response to each question, and asks each participant to describe the MAPS process in one word at the end of the planning session. Figure 6.1 provides a summary of MAPS.

The MAPS process has been used by middle school teachers to address team goals. Rather than focusing the MAPS questions on an individual student, they used the process to focus on their team. Using

Eight Key Questions:

Question 1.   What is a MAP?
Question 2.   What is the story of the person or organization?
Question 3.   What is the dream of the person or organization?
Question 4.   What is the nightmare of the person or organization?
Question 5.   Who is the person or organization?
Question 6.   What are the strengths, talents, and unique gifts?
Question 7.   What do we need to do to make the dream happen?
Question 8.   What is the plan of action to avoid the nightmare and to make the dream come true?

FIGURE 6.1   MAPS (Making Action Plans)

From Forest, M., and Pearpoint, J.C. (1992). "Putting All Kids on the MAP." *Educational Leadership* 50(2): 26–31, and Forest, M., and Pearpoint, J.C. (1992). *Inclusion Papers.* Inclusion Press. Reprinted with permission of the Association for Supervision and Curriculum Development. Copyright © 1992 by ASCD. All rights reserved.

MAPS, the team reached consensus on how to avoid the team's nightmares and make dreams come true for their middle school programs.

BARRIERS TO AND SUPPORTS FOR THE TEAMING MODEL

Barriers to Teaming

Barriers to effective interdisciplinary networking among professionals have been listed by Nevin, Thousand, Paolucci-Whitcomb, and Villa (1990). They include the following:

- Lack of planning
- Lack of training
- Lack of time
- Lack of common knowledge base
- Hierarchical relationships
- Lack of responsibility or ownership by all
- Large caseloads
- Lack of funding

Similar to the consulting model, a barrier to the teaming model is lack of a common knowledge base and lack of training for teaming. Similar to the coaching model, a barrier to the teaming model is the hierarchical structure of schools and other human services institutions.

A barrier idiosyncratic to this model is lack of ownership by all team members. In a teaming model, each individual team member must have a vested interest in the team goal and each must share equally in team decisions. If any individual in a group lacks a sense of personal group responsibility and accountability, then the group is not an example of the teaming model of collaboration.

Supports for Teaming

A collaborative team has been described by Thousand and Villa (1992) as a group of people, with a common goal and a shared belief system, who work with parity and distributed functions in a collaborative teaming process. Such a team empowers members through shared ownership of problems and shared decision making with regard to problem solutions. The hallmarks of effective teams include face-to-face interactions, positive interdependence, trust, assessment of team functioning, and individual accountability. Working as a collaborative team can simplify complex issues in education or other human service areas. Participation on such a team can empower the individual with a disability in his/her pursuit of appropriate educational opportunities and his/her efforts ultimately to realize independence.

Successful teaming requires interpersonal communication, problem solving, and evaluation skills (Nevin, Thousand, Paolucci-Whitcomb, and Villa, 1990). Team members should have a knowledge of collaborative teaming examples, and competence in the history, legalities, and rights of students with disabilities.

Essential competencies for teaming were found to fall into nine category clusters by West and Cannon (1988):

- Collaborative theory
- Research on theory, training, and practice
- Personal characteristics
- Interactive communication skill
- Collaborative problem solving
- Systems change
- Equity issues and values/belief systems
- Staff development
- Evaluation of effectiveness

The list compares to competencies listed previously as necessary for the consulting and coaching models. This should come as no surprise since all three models are different types of collaborative practice. Any collaborative effort will be more successful if the participants are trained for

1. Select the Objectives
2. Assign Learners to Groups
3. Arrange the Classroom
4. Provide the Appropriate Materials
5. Set the Task and Goal Structure
6. Monitor the Learner–Learner Interaction
7. Intervene to Solve Problems and Teach Skills
8. Evaluate Outcomes

FIGURE 6.2   Eight Steps toward Cooperative Learning

From Idol, L., Nevin, A., and Paolucci-Whitcomb, P. (1994). *Collaborative Consultation.* Austin, TX: Pro-Ed. Reprinted with permission.

their roles. Personal characteristics such as open-mindedness, acceptance, and flexibility ensure positive individual interactions. Interactive problem solving and ongoing evaluation efforts are hallmarks of effective collaborative practice.

In an analysis of teacher assistance teams, Chalfant and Pysh (1989) identified three major factors as contributing to team effectiveness: (1) principal support; (2) team attributes and performance; and (3) teacher support. They made six recommendations for improving team effectiveness that include administrative support, faculty support, training, team procedures, networking, and evaluation.

Team procedures can be enhanced with use of the same strategies used to promote successful student cooperative learning groups (Idol, Nevin, and Paolucci-Whitcomb, 1994). There are eight basic steps for structuring student groups. Adults working as part of a team should first determine the team's objectives. Provision of a comfortable physical space for team meetings and the necessary materials will enhance both teaming efficiency and eventual effectiveness. As suggested by Thousand and Villa (1992), each team member should develop an awareness of and sensitivity to intra-team personal interactions. Finally, continual self-evaluation of the teaming effort is essential for continued team productivity. These components are outlined in Figure 6.2 as the eight steps toward cooperative learning for "youngsters" of any age.

APPROPRIATE APPLICATION
OF THE TEAMING MODEL

Appropriate Use

The teaming model of collaboration can be an effective means of empowering teachers to accept responsibility for student success and school effectiveness. In order to implement this model, participants must respect the varied expertise of individual team members. The model can be successfully employed by professionals who have reached a level of professional maturity and confidence that allows them to listen to the opinions of peers, weigh those opinions against their own, and continually re-evaluate their own positions. Use of teaming requires shared leadership, goal setting, and decision making.

Step-by-Step Application

Step 1—team focus. For the teaming model to be effectively implemented, the team members should state a team vision, goal, or purpose. Although individual members may have their personal agendas as well, when working as team members, their agenda has to be that of the team.

Step 2—role sharing. Team roles include a team leader or facilitator, a team recorder, team reporter, and team observer. Different members of a team have expertise in different areas, but no one member should always play the same role. The team leader or facilitator maintains team focus at the team meeting. Depending upon the team's meeting objective, the member with expertise in the topic under discussion may be the most appropriate leader. As the purpose of team interactions changes, so should the leadership. The team recorder takes minutes of the team's activity. The reporter should be available to disseminate information with regard to team activity and progress to the school or organization as a whole. The team observer plays a very important team role. The observer takes notes about the team process itself. This role is especially important for team evaluation and should be shared so that different perceptions of the team are available for review.

Step 3—individual accountability. Unless a team is composed of two members, as in a co-teaching situation, it is easy as an individual to avoid responsibility. Assigning specific roles during a team meeting and assigning specific tasks to individuals for completion between team meetings assures individual accountability. For the teaming model to be optimally effective, each individual team member has to share responsibility for achieving team goals.

Step 4—team processing. In the consulting model, self-evaluation on the part of the consultant is essential for assessing effectiveness. In the coaching model, dyad reflection serves as the evaluative component. For effective collaboration using the teaming model, group processing serves as the team critique. Individually and together team members can review and analyze the observer notes and discuss the team process. Through this form of professional dialogue, the team can monitor itself and adjust the way the team does business in order to develop into an effective and efficient interactive team.

Application of Clinical Observation

As in the other models of collaboration, clinical observation serves as a basic tool for the teaming model. Teachers who are co-teaching can use the preconference–observation–postconference sequence to observe and coach each other into an example of true team teaching. Similarly, teachers who use this model for professional development will have to employ clinical observation if their focus is on in-class instructional improvement. In the teaming examples involving collaboration across agencies, clinical observation can be used by employees of different organizations to observe and gain an understanding of the different institutions' intent, purpose, and daily operating procedures. If teaming is used for problem solving, clinical observation forms a basis for gaining objective data about students in order to meet their individual and group educational needs.

SUMMARY

This chapter has presented the teaming model of collaboration. Teaming has been defined as an interactive process involving equal levels but different areas of expertise on the parts of individual team members and the willingness of members to share authority with each other. Examples of teaming have been provided in co-teaching, professional development and appraisal, and problem solving. Finally, barriers to and supports for teaming have been discussed, along with the appropriate use of the teaming model.

VIGNETTE REPRISE

The teaming model of collaboration was the perfect model for meeting Nick's needs. Community inclusion requires support from all sides. The friends who were supporting Nick each had the capability of offering their support in a different area. Several members of the team visited Nick on Saturday morning to assist with housekeeping chores, make a weekly shopping list, and accompany Nick to the grocery store. Another took charge of Nick's finances and helped him deposit weekly paychecks, balance his checkbook, and determine a weekly spending allowance. One team member prompted Nick to take medication regularly and to check his calendar for medical, dental, or counseling appointments. Two of the group members who were long-time family friends reminded Nick to phone home to talk with his parents and made sure that he had ample postage available for

*cards and letters. Each member of the "Friends-of-Nick" team shared own-
ership of the group efforts to support Nick's continued community inclusion, each was more competent in one area or another for supporting his
independent living, and all shared with Nick in decision making for his current and future needs.*

PORTFOLIO ACTIVITIES

1. *Personal Application:* Use the MAPS process with a student, his/her family,
   and friends. How did the participants feel about the process? How can the
   MAP be applicable to school programming or post-school living?

2. *Professional Reflection:* Bradford (1986) describes the Metropolitan
   Teaching Effectiveness Cadre as if it were a team. Is the cadre an interactive team as we have described it? Why or why not? If you think that it is
   an example of teaming, defend your response. If you think that the cadre
   is not an example of a teaming model, how could it be modified in order
   to qualify?

3. *Action Research:* Survey five schools in one urban district and one school in
   five rural districts with regard to their prereferral to the special education
   process. Ask the following questions:

   • Is there a prereferral process in place in your school?
   • Who are the members of the prereferral team? Why is the team com-
     position the way it is?
   • Describe the prereferral process.
   • Have data been kept on the comparative numbers of students referred
     to special education before and after implementing prereferral? (If the
     data are available, chart it.)

   Can you come to any conclusions or make any generalizations based upon
   your survey?

REFERENCES

Bickel, W.E., and Artz, N.J. (1984). "Improving Instruction through Focused
    Team Supervision." *Educational Leadership* 41(7): 22–23.
Bradford, D. (1986). "The Metropolitan Teaching Effectiveness Cadre."
    Educational Leadership 43(5): 53–55.
Chalfant, J.C., and Pysh, M.V. (1989). "Teacher Assistance Teams: Five Descriptive
    Studies on 96 Teams." *RASE: Remedial and Special Education* 10(6): 49–58.
Donaldson, G.A., Jr. (1993). "Working Smarter Together." *Educational Leadership*
    51(2): 12–16.

Donaldson, R., and Christiansen, J. (1990). "Consultation and Collaboration: A Decision Making Model." *Teaching Exceptional Children* 22(2): 22–25.

Forest, M., and Lusthaus, E. (1990). "Everyone Belongs." *Teaching Exceptional Children* 22(2): 32–35.

Forest, M., and Pearpoint, J.C. (1992). "Putting All Kids on the MAP." *Educational Leadership* 50(2): 26–31.

Friend, M., and Cook, L. (November 1994). "Co-Teaching: Principles, Practices, and Pragmatics." Paper presented at the annual conference of the Council for Learning Disabilities, San Diego.

Gallivan-Fenlon, A. (1994). "Integrated Transdisciplinary Teams." *Teaching Exceptional Children* 26(3): 16–21.

Glatthorn, A.A. (1987). "Cooperative Professional Development: Peer-Centered Options for Teacher Growth." *Educational Leadership* 45(3): 31–35.

Graden, J.L. (1989). "Redefining 'Prereferral' Intervention as Intervention Assistance: Collaboration between General and Special Education." *Exceptional Children* 56(3): 227–231.

Idol, L., Nevin, A., and Paolucci-Whitcomb, P. (1994). *Collaborative Consultation*, 2d ed. Austin, TX: Pro-Ed.

Johnson, D.W., and Johnson, R.T. (1987). "Research Shows the Benefits of Adult Cooperation." *Educational Leadership* 45(3): 27–30.

Krovetz, M., and Cohick, D. (1993). "Professional Collegiality Can Lead to School Change." *Phi Delta Kappan* 75(4): 331–333.

Morsink, C.V., Thomas, C.C., and Correa, V.I. (1991). *Interactive Teaming: Consultation and Collaboration in Special Programs*. New York: Merrill-Macmillan Publishing Co.

Nelson, B.S. (1986). "Collaboration for Colleagueship: A Program in Support of Teachers." *Educational Leadership* 43(5): 50–52.

Nevin, A., Thousand, J., Paolucci-Whitcomb, P., and Villa, R. (1990). "Collaborative Consultation: Empowering Public School Personnel to Provide Heterogeneous Schooling for All—Or, Who Rang that Bell?" *Journal of Educational and Psychological Consultation* 1(1): 41–67.

Paquette, M. (1987). "Voluntary Collegial Support Groups for Teachers." *Educational Leadership* 45(3): 36–39.

Pugach, M.C., and Johnson, L.J. (1989). "Prereferral Interventions: Progress, Problems and Challenges." *Exceptional Children* 56(3): 217–226.

Redditt, S. (1991). "Two Teachers Working as One: Co-Teaching for Special/Regular Education Integration." *Equity and Choice* 8(1): 49–56.

Sharan, Y., and Sharan, S. (1987). "Training Teachers for Cooperative Learning." *Educational Leadership* 45(3): 20–26.

Sweeney, J., and Manatt, D. (1984). "A Team Approach to Supervising the Marginal Teacher." *Educational Leadership* 41(7): 25–27.

Thousand, J.S., and Villa, R.A. (1992). "Collaborative Teams: A Powerful Tool in School Restructuring." In R. Villa, J. Thousand, W. Stainback, and S. Stainback, (eds.), *Restructuring for Caring and Effective Education*. Baltimore: Paul H. Brookes Publishing Co.

Vandercook, T., York, J., and Forest, M. (1989). "The McGill Action Planning System (MAPS): A Strategy for Building the Vision." *JASH* 14(3): 205–215.

Welch, M., Judge, J., Anderson, J., Bray, J., Child, B., and Franke, L. (1990). "COOP: A Tool for Implementing Prereferral Consultation." *Teaching Exceptional Children* 22(2): 30–31.

West, J.F., and Cannon, G.S. (1988). "Essential Collaborative Consultation Competencies for Regular and Special Educators." *Journal of Learning Disabilities* 21(1): 56–63.

West, J.F., and Idol, L. (1990). "Collaborative Consultation in the Education of Mildly Handicapped and At-Risk Students." *RASE: Remedial and Special Education* 11(1): 22–31.

7

PURPOSES OF COLLABORATION

Vignette

As Sarah prepared for her master's comprehensive examination, she studied her class notes, did additional reading at the university library, and reflected on her experiences. She pondered the many uses of the different collaboration models to which she had been exposed. After reading an article by Garmston (1987) in an issue of Educational Leadership, *she attempted to categorize the ways in which she had been collaborating. She thought about examples of collaborative practice that had been discussed in class and attempted to discern their purposes. Focused on teacher peer coaching, the article had described three coaching forms—technical, collegial, and challenge. Sarah thought about her work with Marissa. As Marissa's job coach, part of Sarah's role involved building in her own obsolescence. Sarah would fade as a continuing support for Marissa, as she taught the motel manager and lead housekeeper to be job coaches for the young woman. Sarah was using the consulting model for the purpose of offering technical assistance. Sarah also thought about Danny. Her thoughts often strayed to this difficult young man. He had such a sensitive inner core, and such a blustery surface. She and her friend had been engaging in the coaching model with the weekday house parents for the purpose of collegial support. When Danny showed his temper, everyone involved required support. Sarah thought about Nick's mother and the team of friends upon whom she was counting to make independent living a reality for her son. Although the team met on a regular monthly basis, one or all of the team members met more often, either in person or by phone, for crisis intervention. They used the teaming model for challenge solutions. As Sarah continued to review, to analyze, and to synthesize all of the information and experiences garnered during her graduate studies, she wondered about application of the different peer coaching purposes, as proposed by Garmston, to the three basic collaboration models.*

Chapter Outline

PURPOSES FOR COLLABORATIVE PRACTICE

Since the passage of P.L. 94-142, The Education of All Handicapped Children Act (EHA) in 1975, with its least restrictive environment (LRE) clause, more and more children with special learning needs have been educated with their nondisabled peers in the general education main-stream. This law's most recent revision, the Individuals with Disabilities Education Act (IDEA), signed in 1990, reinforced the LRE. Case law, as established by district, appellate, and Supreme Court decisions has extended the LRE concept to the inclusion of any child with any type or severity of disability in education's mainstream, if that inclusion is at all possible (*Board of Education v. Rowley*, 1982; *Board of Education of Sacramento U.S.D. v. Holland*, 1992; *Daniel R.R. v. State Board of Education*, 1989; *Honig v. Doe*, 1988; *Irving I.S.D. v. Tatro*, 1984; *Oberti v. Clementon Board of Education*, 1993). Programming for children with a wide range of physical, academic, and social abilities demands that teachers, whether they have been trained as special or general educators, work together. Inclusive educational practice demands teacher collaboration. Inclusion has become the focus of most collaborative practice in the educational system.

As students mature, the emphasis shifts from providing educational opportunities to transitioning students from school to work environments. P.L. 99-457 (1986), although most frequently cited for its preschool provisions, also mandated provision of individual transition plans beginning when a student reaches sixteen years of age. IDEA has reinforced this mandate. A major goal of inclusive educational practice is preparing students for participation in a diverse culture. Consideration of transition issues eases an individual student's rite of passage from school to a post-school environment. Collaboration between the schools and community service agencies to address transition issues is increasing.

Quality of life after school then becomes an issue (Ferguson and Ferguson, 1993). To what are students being transitioned? Hopefully, they are leaving school to lead productive lives. If diversity is truly valued, the extension of school inclusion means workplace inclusion of persons with significant disabling conditions. School inclusion should be preparation for productive citizenship. For individuals to lead as independent and productive lives as possible, regardless of ability or disability, collaboration among many individuals and agencies becomes imperative. Community inclusion cannot happen unless the person with the disability and all components of their support system work together. Support for their community inclusion has become the focus of collaboration among professionals, family, and friends of persons with a wide range of disabilities.

For educators, training in collaborative strategies appears to be increasing. Both undergraduate and graduate courses address the issue of collaboration. In addition, school districts often request collaboration training for their inservice teachers' continuing professional development. College faculty may offer this training as an off-campus course or on a consultative basis. The training may include information on the legal basis for inclusive practice and the ensuing need for collaboration (Chapter 2), consideration of adult development and types of leadership appropriate to developmental levels (Chapter 8), analysis of both stages and components of the change process (Chapter 9), and provision of a structure for collaborative practice (Chapters 4, 5, and 6).

Collaboration means working together for a common end. Perhaps the most important component of training for collaboration is provision of collaboration models that teachers can employ along with a rationale for appropriate use. With this information, teachers and other human services professionals can analyze a particular situation, choose the best model for that situation, and evaluate the effectiveness of their collaborative practice. This same training is applicable to the professionals who will be providing community inclusion opportunities for individuals as they leave the safety and consistency of a school environment.

In a discussion of peer coaching, Garmston (1987) suggests three ways in which teachers coach each other. The first is technical assistance. Teachers seek advice from each other for individual student programming. The second is collegial coaching. Teachers provide feedback to each other in terms of professional development activities and goals. The third is challenge coaching. Teachers assist each other in solving immediate challenging or problem situations. Although Garmston proposes these three types of interaction for the peer coaching model only, his premise applies to a much broader arena.

In fact, the purpose of any collaborative effort can be described in one of these three ways. The consulting model may have as its purpose technical assistance, collegial support, or challenge solution. In Chapter 4, examples of consulting fell into three categories. The first was mentoring. Mentor programs are developed to provide moral support and technical assistance to novice teachers. Most mentors serve as consultants for the purpose of offering technical assistance to their protégés. The examples of the consulting model for student support could have as their purpose challenge solutions. The programs were developed to meet the individual chronic and acute challenges posed by special education students. Interagency consultation may be viewed in terms of collegial support. In the example of university personnel working with professional development schools, higher education faculty supported PDS faculty in reflection, experimentation, informal study, and curriculum restructuring.

Likewise, the purpose of coaching or teaming model implementation may be technical assistance, collegial support, or challenge solution. Examples of coaching applied to performance appraisal exemplify use of coaching for technical assistance. When coaching is employed for professional development of the coaching partners, its purpose is collegial support. The initiator–facilitator dyads proposed in Chapter 5 as an intervention strategy for at-risk students is an example of coaching for challenge solutions. Likewise, the purpose of teaming can be for technical assistance, professional development, or challenge solution. Co-teaching teams promote team members' technical improvement and expertise. Teaming has been used in the form of teacher study groups to support individual professional growth. Teacher assistance teams (TATs) are a common form of teaming for solving student challenges. Figure 7.1 summarizes the interaction of the three collaboration models with these three purposes.

COLLABORATION FOR TECHNICAL ASSISTANCE

Garmston (1987) describes technical coaching as helping teachers to transfer training to classroom practice. The technical assistance purpose of any model of collaboration has broader implications than the

		MODEL		
		Consulting	**Coaching**	**Teaming**
PURPOSE	**Technical Assistance**	Consulting Assistance	Coaching Assistance	Teaming Assistance
	Collegial Support	Consulting Support	Coaching Support	Teaming Support
	Challenge Solution	Consulting Solution	Coaching Solution	Teaming Solution

FIGURE 7.1   Purposes for Models of Collaboration

classroom setting. Technical assistance is the purpose of collaboration in any area of education or the human services when one party requires the technical expertise of another. This purpose is easy to pair with the consulting model but may not at first be easily discerned as appropriate for the coaching and teaming models.

Volumes have been devoted to consulting for technical assistance. Heron and Harris (1993) describe the educational consultant's process and role in terms of technical assistance regarding students, parents, elementary and secondary curricula and instruction, assessment, and behavior management. Sugai and Tindal (1993) focus their text on technical assistance in terms of behavioral theory and implementation. Idol (1993) provides an in-depth guide for teachers who serve a resource and consulting technical assistance role. The first edition of *Collaborative Consultation* (Idol, Paolucci-Whitcomb, and Nevin, 1987) is devoted to development of the technical assistance role of an educational consultant. While technical assistance may be obviously compatible with the consulting model, it can be the purpose of collaboration in either the coaching or teaming models as well. Examples of technical assistance as the purpose of each of the three basic models of collaboration are provided below.

Consulting Model

In the Chapter 4 vignette, Sarah assumed the role of job coach for a young woman named Marissa. As Marissa's job coach, Sarah served as a consultant to the motel employer. Sarah's activities with regard to teaching the motel manager and lead housekeeper are examples of a technical purpose. Sarah might develop a mainstream consultation agreement as described by Tindal et al. (1987). (See Chapter 4, section: "Consulting for Student Support"). The agreement would specify expectations of both Sarah and the motel staff for Marissa and would outline criteria for judging Marissa's job performance. Sarah, the lead housekeeper, and Marissa would agree upon their individual responsibilities as consultant, mentor, and apprentice. With this MCA, the job coach would offer ongoing technical assistance to motel personnel as they learned to provide the support needed for Marissa's continued employment.

Coaching Model

In Chapter 5, Sarah accepted the additional responsibility of a weekend house parent in a group home. Danny, one of the group home residents, had an unpredictable temper. He was often irritable and had great difficulty adapting to change. Sarah and the weekday parents began coaching each other in implementing a problem-solving approach to Danny's behavior. In the framework of peer clinical supervision (McFaul and Cooper, 1984) (see Chapter 5, section: "Coaching for Professional Development"), and using clinical observation, they observed each other working through the four-step initiator–facilitator process as described by Johnson, Pugach, and Cook (1993). (See Chapter 5, section: "Coaching for Problem Solving.") The coaching pairs debriefed with each other on their ability to describe a problem, refine their descriptions through the use of clarifying questions, strategize and implement the chosen strategy, then evaluate effectiveness of their chosen plan. Each team provided anecdotal data recorded during plan implementation while the other team was not present. Sarah knew the clinical model and initiator–facilitator process better than did the weekday house parents. She provided technical assistance by coaching their developing expertise.

Teaming Model

Nick, the young man described in Chapter 6, had the luxury of a team of friends to support his efforts toward independent living. Each of the team members had their own professional expertise and each would take the lead in that area of Nick's supported living. One member, a psychiatric social worker, worked with Nick's counselor and led the team in supporting Nick through the loss he felt as a result of his parents' move. Another was a banker who led the team in supporting Nick as he learned basic money management skills. Supporting Nick's independent living required continuing attention of the team to technical adjustments and adaptations in the transdisciplinary manner described by Gallivan-Fenlon (1994). (See Chapter 6, section: "Teaming as Co-Teaching.")

COLLABORATION FOR COLLEGIAL SUPPORT

Garmston (1987) describes collegial coaching as refining teaching practices, deepening collegiality, increasing professional dialogue, and promoting self-reflection. Project Class (Gallacher, 1995) promotes coaching relationships among individuals and agencies working with young children with disabilities for supporting early intervention efforts. West, Idol, and Cannon (1989) have developed an extensive in-service package devoted to the communication, interaction, and problem-solving skills necessary for collegially supportive collaborative relationships. Collegial support as a purpose of collaboration can be easily related to the Coaching Model, but applies to the consulting and teaming models as well. Examples follow.

Consulting Model

Sarah, as the job coach, might work specifically with the motel manager as she learned first to tolerate and eventually to accept Marissa as an employee. Acting in a role similar to a rural extension agent as described by McIntosh and Raymond (1988) (see Chapter 4, section: "Interagency Consulting"), Sarah demonstrated prompting, cueing, and other job-coaching strategies. As an expert in the field of supported employment, Sarah could provide information and resources to the manager as she developed the skills and insights needed to be a supported employer.

Coaching Model

For the purpose of collegial support, Danny's house parents observed each other, collected data, and assisted with data analysis focusing on house parent skill with the problem-solving process. The process was similar to the peer evaluation project described by Anastos and Ancowitz (1987). (See Chapter 5, section: "Coaching for Professional Development.") Those involved used the clinical observation cycle, as well as videotapes in their efforts to assist each other in problem solving with Danny. Data demonstrated increasing proficiency on the part of Sarah and the weekday house parents in approaching behavioral difficulties from a problem-solving perspective. Through this activity, Sarah achieved the objectives of her course in severe disabilities using the coaching model with the purpose of collegial support.

Teaming Model

Nick's team decided to assist each other in learning more about his disabilities. They devoted one weekly meeting each month to discussion of a recent book, article, or television report addressing developmental disabilities in general or autism in particular. The group worked through Paquette's (1987) (see Chapter 6, section: "Teaming as Support for Professional Development") three phases of team building, learning and application, and reporting successes. As a team, they decided how to use what they had learned with Nick, and how they could support each other in this application.

COLLABORATION FOR CHALLENGE SOLUTIONS

Challenge coaching is described by Garmston (1987) as helping teams to resolve chronic instructional problems or an acute problematic state. It is assumed that team problem solving will produce thoughtful and practical instructional improvements. Team collaboration for meeting educational challenges has been described in detail in both *Interactive Teaming* (Morsink, Thomas, and Correa, 1991) and the second edition of *Collaborative Consultation* (Idol, Nevin, and Paolucci-Whitcomb, 1994). As with the technical assistance and collegial support purposes for collaboration, challenge solution can be the purpose of each of the three collaborative models. Examples of challenge solution as a purpose in each of the three models are described below.

Consulting Model

Marissa often came to work looking disheveled with oily, unwashed hair. Utilizing brief strategic intervention (Amatea, 1990) (see Chapter 4, section: "Consulting for Student Support"), Sarah met with the lead housekeeper to suggest past strategies which had been successful in encouraging Marissa to take more pride in her appearance. The BSI approach involves identifying key elements in the behavioral problem, proposing a solution different from past efforts, developing specific action steps, and monitoring change.

Coaching Model

One Friday morning, in anticipation of the coming weekend changes, Danny became so overwrought that he began tearing up the Friday morning editions rather than folding them and stuffing them in the protective plastic covers. The weekday house parents asked Sarah and her friend to come a day early in order to coach them through the current crises behavior using Johnson, Pugach, and Cook's four steps (1993). (See Chapter 5, section: "Coaching for Problem Solving.")

Teaming Model

Nick continually forgot to take his medication. Without it, his attention to task deteriorated making his job performance at a local restaurant less than acceptable. Nick's team met to discuss strategies for maintaining consistency in medication. They had to decide whether consistent prompts to Nick would increase medication use, if he should take his medication when he arrived at work rather than being responsible for it at home, or if one of the team should make it a point to stop in each day to administer the medication on a regular schedule. The team considered components of teamwork as outlined by Thousand and Villa (1990; 1992) in order to be most effective. (See Chapter 6, section: "Supports for Teaming.")

SUMMARY

Collaboration among educators and among human services professionals and collaboration between the educational and human services institutions is essential in an age of community inclusion. No one individual nor single service institution can adequately serve the needs of an increasingly complex society. Collaboration in the form of consulting, coaching, or teaming for the purpose of technical assistance, collegial support, or challenge solution will permit and facilitate more efficient and effective service delivery across human service organizations.

VIGNETTE REPRISE

As Sarah's head swam with the combinations and permutations of models and purposes, she became more and more excited. What a wealth of possibilities this information offered her for application in Blue Spruce! Sarah began to devise a method for recording her collaborative practice, categorizing the type of each interaction and analyzing the outcomes so that she could become more effective as a collaborative professional.

PORTFOLIO ACTIVITIES

1. *Personal Application:* Use the action research activity in number 3 to analyze your professional collaboration. Think of each collaborative interaction in terms of type, purpose, and outcome. Was the type of interaction best suited to the purpose? Did the outcome of each interaction result from the relationship between type and purpose? Could outcomes have been better if type and purpose had been better focused? Explain.

	MODEL		
	Consulting	**Coaching**	**Teaming**
Technical Assistance	Date Result	Date Result	Date Result
Collegial Support	Date Result	Date Result	Date Result
Challenge Solution	Date Result	Date Result	Date Result

PURPOSE (vertical label on left side)

FIGURE 7.2   Collaboration Analysis Record

2. *Professional Reflection:* Read the article on which this chapter is based (Garmston, 1987). Analyze one example of the consulting model (Ch. 4), the coaching model (Ch. 5), and the teaming model (Ch. 6) in terms of Garmston's three purposes—technical assistance, collegial support, or challenge solution. Can you find an application of each purpose for each model?

3. *Action Research:* As a resource teacher, maintain the Collaborative Analysis Record (Figure 7.2) for a month. Record each collaborative interaction and its outcome according to model and purpose. Answer the following questions based on charted interactions:

- What type(s) of collaboration do you use most frequently?
- What is the most frequent purpose for your collaboration?
- Was the outcome of each collaborative endeavor positive (+) or negative (–)?

REFERENCES

Amatea, E.S. (1990). "Shifting the School's Solution: Using Brief Strategic Intervention in Teacher Consultation." *Special Services in the Schools* 6(1–2): 81–98.

Anastos, J., and Ancowitz, R. (1987). "A Teacher-Directed Peer Coaching Project." *Educational Leadership* 45(3): 40–42.

Board of Education of Sacramento U.S.D v. Holland, 786 F. Supp. 847 (E.D. Cal., 1992).

Board of Education v. Rowley, 458 U.S. 176, 102 S.Ct. 3034, 73 L.Ed. 2d 690 (1982).

Daniel R.R. v. State Board of Education, 874 F. 2d 1036 (5th Cir. 1989).

Education of All Handicapped Children Act of 1975. P.L. 94-142. U.S.C. §1401 (1975).

Education of All Handicapped Children Act, Amended 1986. P.L. 99-457. U.S.C. §1422 (1986).

Ferguson, P., and Ferguson, D. (1993). "The Promise of Adulthood." In M.E. Snell (ed.), *Systematic Instruction of Persons with Severe Handicaps,* 4th ed. New York: Merrill, an imprint of Macmillan Publishing Co.

Gallacher, K. (1995). *Coaching Partnerships: Refining Early Intervention Practices.* University of Montana: Project Class.

Gallivan-Fenlon, A. (1994). "Integrated Transdisciplinary Teams." *Teaching Exceptional Children* 26(3): 16–21.

Garmston, R.J. (1987). "How Administrators Support Peer Coaching." *Educational Leadership* 44(5): 18–26.

Heron, T.E., and Harris, K.C. (1993). *The Educational Consultant.* Austin, TX: Pro-Ed.

Honig v. Doe, 484 U.S. 108, S.Ct. 592, 98 L.Ed. 2d 686 (1988).

Idol, L. (1993). *Special Educator's Consultation Handbook.* Austin, TX: Pro-Ed.

Idol, L., Nevin, A., and Paolucci-Whitcomb, P. (1994). *Collaborative Consultation,* 2d ed. Austin, TX: Pro-Ed.

Idol, L., Paolucci-Whitcomb, P., and Nevin, A (1987). *Collaborative Consultation.* Austin, TX: Pro-Ed.

Individuals with Disabilities Education Act. P.L. 101-476. U.S.C. §§1401–1468 (1990).

Irving I.S.D. v. Tatro, 468 U.S. 883, 104 S.Ct. 3371, 82 L.Ed. 2d 664 (1984).

Johnson, L.J., Pugach, M.C., and Cook, R. (1993). "Peer Collaboration as a Means to Facilitate Collegial Support to Reduce Teacher Isolation and Facilitate Classroom Problem Solving in Rural Areas." *Rural Special Education Quarterly* 12: 21–26.

McFaul, S., and Cooper, J.M. (1984). "Peer Clinical Supervision: Theory vs. Reality." *Educational Leadership* 41: 4–9.

McIntosh, D.K., and Raymond, G.I. (1988). "A Consultation Model for Rural Schools." *Rural Educator* 9(2): 19–21.

Morsink, C.V., Thomas, C.C., and Correa, V.I. (1991). *Interactive Teaming: Consultation and Collaboration in Special Programs.* New York: Merrill, an imprint of Macmillan Publishing Co.

Oberti v. Clementon Board of Education, 995 F. 2d 1204 (3d Cir. 1993).

Paquette, M. (1987). "Voluntary Collegial Support Groups for Teachers." *Educational Leadership* 45(3): 36–39.

Sugai, G.M., and Tindal, G.A. (1993). *Effective School Consultation.* Pacific Grove, CA: Brooks/Cole Publishing Co.

Thousand, J.S., and Villa, R.A. (1990). "Sharing Expertise and Responsibilities through Teaching Teams." In W. Stainback, and S. Stainback (eds.), *Support Networks for Inclusive Schooling.* Baltimore: Paul H. Brookes Publishing Co.

Thousand, J.S., and Villa, R.A. (1992). "Collaborative Teams: A Powerful Tool in School Restructuring." In R.A. Villa, J.S. Thousand, W. Stainback and S. Stainback (eds.), *Restructuring for Caring and Effective Education.* Baltimore: Paul H. Brookes Publishing Co.

Tindal, G., Shinn, M., Walz, L., and German, G. (1987). "Mainstream Consultation in Secondary Settings: The Pine County Model." *Journal of Special Education* 21(3): 94–106.

West, J.F., Idol, L., and Cannon, G. (1989). *Collaboration in the Schools.* Austin, TX: Pro-Ed.

8

IMPACT OF ADULT DEVELOPMENT
AND SITUATIONAL LEADERSHIP

Vignette

After passing her master's comprehensives, Sarah began the second year of her graduate program and began to work in earnest on her thesis. Because several graduate students had completed their degrees, Sarah was offered the opportunity of supervising undergraduate students in field experiences. The university had three major field components for education majors—a sophomore practicum, a junior field methods experience, and senior student teaching. Because as an undergraduate Sarah had only student taught, and because she wanted to understand all three program components, she agreed to supervise nine students, three at each level. She quickly learned that supervision was not supervision was not supervision! Sarah adjusted her style of supervision to meet the individual needs of her nine students. Not only was she working with nine different individuals, but each of them was at a different adult developmental and career developmental stage from the others.

One of the sophomores was a nontraditional student who had been working as a classroom assistant in the Plainsview schools for twelve years. She knew how to manage a classroom, how to meet the needs of diverse learners, and had experience at a variety of grade levels. She was a mature individual who had decided it was time to earn her baccalaureate degree and a teaching certificate. The other two sophomores were recent high school graduates. One had no experience at all in schools, other than being a student himself. The other had served as a peer tutor throughout school, worked in after-school recreational programs, and was employed during the summer in a local child care facility.

The junior level supervisees were all traditional students who had successfully completed their sophomore practicum and were attempting to implement in public school classrooms the strategies they were learning in methods courses.

Two of the students were elementary education majors; the third was a secondary education English major. The secondary education major saw no reason for taking the one methods course required of him. He felt strongly that if he had a strong foundation in his academic discipline, he would be able to instill his love of English literature in fifteen-year-old high school sophomores. He perceived the study of pedagogy and formal lesson planning as wasted effort.

Sarah's student teachers were equally challenging. One was a double general-special education major and had completed a semester of general education student teaching. She was familiar with the school, knew her students well, and had demonstrated skill and professional knowledge well beyond her youth and inexperience. The other two students were just beginning their student teaching. They were impatient to graduate and secure teaching positions of their own. They felt that they needed little guidance and less supervision, however, it was apparent to their public school mentors and to Sarah that each had much to learn about professional behavior.

Sarah had her hands full. She had expected to make an initial visit with each student, explain the clinical observation process, and watch them grow. She had not anticipated such diversity in such a small group. She knew little about adult developmental stages and less about situational leadership. Sarah discovered that children are easy to work with; after all, we expect children to be children. We expect adults to act with maturity; only most adults are just big kids!

Chapter Outline

Vignette

Chapter Outline

Chapter Content

    Impact of Development and Leadership on Collaboration
    Adult Development
        Cognitive Development
        Moral Development
        Life Stages
    Career Development
        General Career Development
        Teacher Career Development
    Situational Leadership
        Organizational Development
        Supervisory Style
        Leadership Style
        Bases of Power
        Preparation for Leadership

IMPACT OF DEVELOPMENT AND LEADERSHIP ON COLLABORATION

Often the best attempts at collaboration fail. Knowing the basic models of collaboration, specifying the purpose of the collaborative effort, and understanding the relationship between the two can facilitate successful collaboratives. Even with these pieces in place, however, participants in a collaborative model with the same stated purpose may not be communicating. The situation is analogous to playing the same game, with the same goal, but on different game boards. Just as the players may not realize that they are playing different versions of the same game, the collaborators may fail to understand that they have come into the collaborative endeavor from different perspectives. This chapter addresses adult development and situational leadership—factors to consider in order to promote effective collaborative interactions.

ADULT DEVELOPMENT

As educators, it is easy for us to work with children. We understand the developmental stages through which children pass, and we meet our students on their terms. We expect adults, however, to act according to our preconceived notions of maturity. We fail to consider adult stages of development in our interactions with co-workers. Adults are not finished products. On the contrary, individuals continue to develop throughout their life stages. Two areas of adult development, cognition and morality, are discussed because of their impact on collaboration. These stages are summarized and compared in Figure 8.1.

Cognitive Development

Glickman (1990; 1995) discusses the orderly progression of adult cognitive development. Just as children develop through certain stages, so adults pass through common stages of growth. These stages are in order. The rate of progression, however, varies from one adult to another. Adult

ADULT			**CAREER**	
Cognitive	**Moral**	**Life**	**General**	**Teacher**
Fluid Quick Short-term memory	*Preconventional* Punishment Relativism	*Young Adult* Omnipotence Immortality Dreams	Pre-service Induction	Concern for self
	Conventional Good boy/girl Law and order	*Middle Adult* Expansion Competence Career success	Competence Growth	Concern about technique
Chrystalized Thoughtful Relationships based on experience	*Postconventional* Social contract Universal principles	*Older Adult* Reflection Acceptance Inner order	Frustration Stagnation Wind-down Exit	Concern about impact

(Left margin label spanning rows: STAGES)

FIGURE 8.1   Adult Development Chart

From Glickman, C.D. (1990). *Supervision of Instruction: A Developmental Approach.* Boston: Allyn and Bacon.

From Kohlberg, L. (1995). "The Cognitive-Developmental Approach to Moral Education." In A.C. Ornstein and L.S. Behar (eds.), *Contemporary Issues in Curriculum,* 163–175. Boston: Allyn and Bacon.

From Morsink, C.V., Thomas, C.C., and Correa, V.I. (1991). *Interactive Teaming: Consultation and Collaboration in Special Programs.* New York: Merrill-Macmillan Publishing Co.

learning can be categorized according to fluid learning and crystallized learning. The first type of learning refers to inductive reasoning, figure matching, memory span, and perceptual speed. The second type refers to relationships between experiences. Verbal comprehension, mechanical knowledge, arithmetic ability, fluency of ideas, experiential evaluation, and general information depend upon such relationships. As the nervous system declines with age, so does fluid learning. Instant and visual information can no longer be as easily handled. The comedian, Bill Cosby, does a routine based on increasing loss of short-term memory with age. He elaborates on the experience most of us have had of going from one room to another, only to forget our purpose. Cosby's comic question echoes our own, "Now, what did I come in here for . . . ?" On the other hand, with age comes experience and knowledge on which to base information processing and task completion. Crystallized learning continues to improve throughout most of the adult lifetime. (How exciting for those of us over thirty!)

This information is important for collaboration. As collaborators, young adults will approach collaborative professional interaction from a different cognitive perspective and with different cognitive strengths than will their more mature counterparts. Young adults will grasp new ideas quickly but will have neither the experience for making connections nor the basis for application. More mature professionals, on the other hand, possess a wealth of experience but may require more time for processing and embracing innovative ideas. Old dogs can learn new tricks, but they should be afforded patience as they work through new information.

Moral Development

Kohlberg (1976; 1995) described stages of moral development. The three major stages are preconventional, conventional, and postconventional. Within each major stage are two substages. At the preconventional stage, moral reasoning is very basic. First, individuals do what is right in order to avoid punishment. In a slightly more advanced but still relative stage, individuals do what is right in order to achieve their own ends where others are concerned. The conventional stage is marked by the "good boy/good girl" perspective and by attention to law and order. At the beginning of this developmental stage, individuals are concerned with the opinion of others. By the end, morality is based on self-reinforcement for obeying the law. The postconventional stage is marked by attention to social contract and universal principles. Social contract involves reference to general principles, human rights, and honorable relationships. Finally, the last stage of moral development, achieved by a minority, defines morality in terms of individual conscience. It is based on universal ethical principles, a logical and consistent ethical system, and the dignity of the individual.

While individuals develop from one stage to the next sequentially, the age at which this happens varies from one person to the next. Moral development is dependent upon intellectual development as outlined by Piaget. Usually, very young children at the stage of concrete operations are also at the preconventional stages of moral development. As the individual progresses to formal operational reasoning, they are capable of achieving the conventional moral stages. Research has demonstrated that most people do not progress beyond this stage (Glickman, 1990; 1995; Kohlberg, 1995). Full formal reasoning allows for attainment of postconventional moral development. Kohlberg (1995), however, has found that most people reach a higher logical than moral stage. Our founding fathers were evidently at this stage. The Declaration of Independence, Bill of Rights, and Constitution all reflect a social contract moral developmental level.

Understanding of moral developmental levels will enhance collaborators' awareness of each other's frame of reference. The knowledge of stages in moral development can heighten individual recognition of personal development and can increase understanding of the motivation of other participants in the collaborative efforts. With this heightened understanding, not only will current collaboration have a greater chance of success, but collaborators can even assist each other in further moral development. If educational professionals have reached full formal operations in logical reasoning, then they are capable of achieving the postconventional stages of moral reasoning.

As teachers, most of us have continued in education from preschool through graduate school as students and continue in educational institutions as professionals. Schools tend to be bureaucratically structured with specific conduct rules, role expectations, and time schedules. From the time many educators were four years old, they have been told what to do, when to do it, and how to conduct themselves throughout. Such rigidity leaves little room for reaching a stage of moral maturity based upon fundamental ethical principles. If teachers are to support students as they progress morally, the teachers themselves should have reached a mature moral developmental stage. With understanding of Kohlberg's moral stages, collaborators can support each other's continuing moral progress.

Life Stages

Glickman (1990; 1995) has summarized several theorists with regard to adult life stages. As young adults, we feel omnipotent and eager to have a profound impact on the world, as we live forever. Middle adulthood is marked by expansion, competence, and an eventual reflection on personal limitations and our inevitable mortality. Older adults either come to an acceptance of their lives and a sense of inner order, or they become frustrated and embittered.

Collaborative efforts with individuals at different stages in their lives may have very different results. Young adults who are enthusiastic will be more apt to embrace collaboration in any of its forms. Novice teachers rely on the guidance and support of a mentor in the consulting model. They may be eager to work with peers in the coaching model as they strive to improve their teaching competencies. The teaming model will be a natural outgrowth of the cooperative learning that most students experience in current elementary and secondary school programs.

Collaboration among mature individuals in middle adulthood may promote in-depth professional dialogue and development. Adults at this stage are competent individuals at the peak of their careers. Maturity, competence, a sense of self-worth, and personal confidence are factors that can facilitate and support meaningful collaboration. The consulting model between professional equals who have expertise in different areas need not be threatening or met with resistance. The coaching model can be implemented in more than a superficial manner. The teaming model can result in accomplishments for individual students or for the school at large that are greater than the sum of individual capabilities.

As adults reach later life stages and experience a sense of their personal achievements and acceptance of their life's work, collaboration may become more difficult. Most current educational professionals have been reared in the philosophy of competition and rugged individualism. Collaboration with peers is a new concept. An individual who has achieved inner order may see no need to face the cognitive dissonance necessary for understanding and embracing any educational innovation.

CAREER DEVELOPMENT

Career development can be considered a subset of overall adult development. Like personal cognitive, moral, and life-stage progression, career development is a more-or-less orderly process.

General Career Development

Morsink, Thomas, and Correa (1991) discuss career development in terms of the following stages: pre-service, induction, competency building, enthusiastic growth, frustration, stable/stagnant, wind-down, and exit (Burke, Christensen, and Fessler, 1984). These career stages correlate roughly with life stages. As a young adult bent on changing the world, the individual is in the pre-service and induction phases of their career. Competency, growth, frustration, and stability/stagnation would correspond to middle adulthood. Finally, career wind-down and exit would naturally occur as an older adult. This is not always a direct correlation, however. Often, young adults become easily disillusioned or frustrated with their initial career choice and go through the stages very rapidly, then change careers. Sometimes individuals complete one stage in their life cycle and decide on a career change. Mothers with the "empty nest syndrome" or career military retirees are examples. Having completed one career, these individuals may embark on a new career path. Often they decide to continue the education that they postponed and complete baccalaureate degrees. In any case, an individual's life and career stages may not readily correspond.

Teacher Career Development

Teaching has been found to have a developmental sequence specific to the profession (Fuller, 1969). Novice teachers are concerned about their own competence. They worry about their ability to deliver instruction, as well as to manage a classroom. This self-concern is quite evident in student teachers. These apprentices seek affirmation from their on-site mentors and university supervisors. As new teachers become more personally confident, they begin to worry about their instructional and management techniques. Their concern shifts from concern for self to concern for the act of teaching. It is only after teachers reach a level of teaching maturity that they begin to worry about their impact on the learner. At this optimal stage of development, a teacher's concern is with learning more than with teaching.

Whenever teachers change positions, they recapitulate this progression. For example, a teacher who has taught sixth grade for years may be administratively re-assigned to kindergarten. Persons who have a teaching credential in one area may decide to earn additional teaching endorsements. An example is a general educator who decides to teach in special education or in a Chapter 1 program. To be a school counselor or administrator requires three years of teaching experience in most states, a graduate degree, and training in the additional endorsement area. As individuals transition from their previous role to their new responsibilities, they worry first about personal competence in the new role, later about fulfilling their new responsibilities as well as possible, and lastly about the impact their performance is having on students and/or faculty.

In order to collaborate effectively, an individual collaborator must consider their own as well as the adult development, life stages, and career development of all of the collaborating participants. An omnipotent, "immortal" young adult, with the vision of turning a school system upside down, who attempts to collaborate with an older stable teacher who is approaching career wind-down and exit, will encounter conflict and frustration. In order for collaboration to be effective, each participant must have some understanding and acceptance of the perspectives of the others.

SITUATIONAL LEADERSHIP

Situational leadership refers to choice of the most appropriate leadership style to fit a specific situation. Collaboration involves leadership, whether that leadership be in the form of consulting, coaching, or team leading. Consulting is leading. Coaches take turns in the leadership or follower roles. Team members assume or release leadership responsibilities within the team as appropriate for their individual expertise in any given situation. Being able to employ appropriate forms of leadership in different situations will enhance collaborative efforts. This section also addresses organizational development because different organizational structures lend themselves to different forms of leadership. An understanding of different bases of power is essential for collaborators, because the basis of authority assumed by a leader can promote or stifle collaboration.

Organizational Development

Institutions are organized in fundamentally different ways (Sergiovanni, Burlingame, Coombs, and Thurston, 1987; 1992). The most familiar organizational form is a bureaucracy. This type of institution is defined by a hierarchical structure, specified roles and responsibilities, a strict division of labor, and a rigid chain of command. Bureaucratic organizations developed from the theory of scientific management. The bureaucracy is an answer to inefficiency and duplication of services. Most schools are bureaucracies, modeled after the raw material input–process–output production of industry.

The human relations organization resulted from the increasing dehumanization of bureaucracies. In this type of institution, people are more important than product. In a human relations based organization, it is the well-being and self-concept of each individual that takes precedence over everything else. Schools based on the human relations theory surfaced during the progressive movement of the 1930s and again during the anti-establishment era of the 1960s.

A politically based institution is organized around political factions and ever-changing coalitions. Individuals in such an institution promote their own welfare and ends at any cost. Because no one individual can fully achieve their own goals, temporary coalitions provide only "satisficing" solutions. Conflict is viewed as natural and to be "satisficed" is to achieve at least a partial victory for one's individual cause. In such an organization, no one person ever achieves total victory, however, neither does anyone experience total defeat. School boards exemplify politically organized bodies where school district policy is based on a series of compromises.

The cultural theory of institutional organization refers to schools as mini societies. In the cultural organization, the culture of the institution itself is promoted, developed, fostered, and maintained. Each school has its own mores, common understanding of language, and yearly traditions. In such an institution, the community of the organization itself provides a secure base for institutional members. Employees or students of such a school would request transfers if they could not accept the organizational culture.

A newer conceptualization is that of a learning organization described by Senge (1990) in *The Fifth Discipline*. Learning organizations promote both individual and organizational actualization. The basic premise of a learning organization is that the organization is only as good as the individuals who work within it, but that the organization has the potential of being greater than the sum of its individual parts. This organization of the future will be explored more fully in Chapter 10.

None of these organizational types is good or bad; the theories merely describe different organizational structures. Most institutions while predominantly one type or another, will exhibit some traits from each of the theories. How a school or human service institution is organized may dictate the type of collaboration that is feasible, at least initially. Consultation, with its one-way direction of expert to novice, is compatible with a bureaucracy. Coaching, with its emphasis on role exchange and individual support may be most compatible with a human relations organizational structure. Teaming that involves group compromise and consensus fits neatly with political and culturally based organizations. Proper implementation, however, will allow use of any of the three models in any type of institutional organization. The theory on which the institution is based will likewise impact the type of institutional leadership employed.

Supervisory Style

Supervision was originally for maintaining quality control in institutions. In a bureaucratic sense, as workers got lazy, supervisors were needed in order to ensure both job completion and product quality. As schools evolved into the human relations type of organization, educational supervision has evolved into instructional supervision with the emphasis on personal professional development. Although there is no less emphasis on quality education, there is more emphasis on assisting professionals to become better at what they do.

There is some question as to whether "supervision" is even necessary in professional organizations (Brandt, 1992; Holzman, 1992; Sergiovanni, 1992). Holzman (1992) has envisioned elementary and high schools without the leadership of the principal. In Holzman's utopian elementary, teachers managed the school when the principal left at midyear. They posted central office mandates on the bulletin board in the teachers' lounge, made curricular decisions, and learned to use a computer data base for student information. They continued to rely on the school secretary for clerical assistance. A nonhierarchical secondary school might be more responsive to learner needs as teachers team to manage the school and continually revise the curriculum. Sergiovanni (1992) contends that more supervision is needed in less professionally oriented institutions, but that as educators come to accept professionalism, supervision becomes superfluous. A professional is accountable to their profession, rather than to an individual administrator.

Instructional supervision can be in one of four styles (Glickman, 1990; 1995). Directive control supervision is employed when the supervisor tells the supervisee what is expected, when it is expected, and subsequently inspects the supervisee's work. Directive informational supervision, as the term connotes, is less controlling, but remains directive. The supervisor lays out the ground rules, but allows the supervisee some professional autonomy in following them. A collaborative supervisory style involves parity on the parts of the supervisor and supervisee. They work together to promote the supervisee's professional growth. Finally, the facilitative style of supervision emphasizes the supervisee over the supervisor. In this style, the supervisor asks clarifying questions, provides food for thought, and serves as a sounding board for the professional being supervised. Control in this type of supervision is in the hands of the supervisee; the supervisor is a mirror of performance and a devil's advocate.

As with collaboration models, or organizational structures, none of these styles has value in and of itself. The value of any style comes with appropriate application of the style to suit an individual situation. Each of the styles might be employed in collaboration. For example, a consultant may have to take control if a novice teacher is not familiar with special education rules and regulations. The teacher may have to be told what to do for an IEP, when to do it, and be monitored in the process. A teacher moving from one state to another may need to be told what the new state's special education rules are, but as a veteran may not require the intensive assistance of a first-year teacher. As the supervisor continues to work with the novice, they may begin to collaborate on developing more appropriate IEP goals and objectives and on programmatic changes for individual students. The veteran teacher, who is a newly relocated individual, may need the supervisor to facilitate their enculturation into the new school community and new state expectations.

Misapplication of any supervisory style is counterproductive. Using a facilitative style with a new teacher who requires direction is frustrating for both individuals involved. Employing the directive control or directive informational supervisory styles with competent faculty, however, is insulting to the teachers and can result in resistance or even sabotage of administrative plans, regardless of their worth. When faculty supervise interns in college or university programs, the appropriate type of supervision changes dramatically from undergraduate students to graduate. Undergraduate students who are enrolled in field experiences require directive informational supervision. They want to know what is required of them and on what criteria they will be evaluated. With less than proficient students, a directive control style may be necessary in order to provide the structure to support student success. Graduate students, on the other hand, usually know exactly what they want to accomplish through their internships. They need astute collaborative or facilitative supervision for benchmarking their efforts and keeping them focused on goals.

Leadership Style

Styles of leadership are analogous to supervisory styles. Blake and Mouton (1964) developed their managerial grid that has been reconceptualized by several theorists since the original. Basically, the grid suggests leadership based on task or people orientation. A high-task, low-relationship manager emphasizes production over people. A low-task, high-relationship manager emphasizes people over production. A high-task, high-relationship manager is focused on both the importance of doing the job, as well as individual employee well-being. The mid-task, mid-relationship manager balances both task and people. The low-task, low-relationship manager is concerned with neither aspect of the workplace. In fact, low-task, low-relationship management is abdication of leadership.

As with supervisory styles, leadership style itself has no value. It is in the appropriate application of leadership that the style gains value. Directive control supervisors could be considered high-task, low-relationship leaders; they tell. Directive informational supervisors might be mid-task, mid-relationship leaders; they re-educate. High-task, high-relationship leaders correspond to collaborative supervisors; they persuade or sell. Low-task, high-relationship leaders are facilitative supervisors; they delegate. In this case, because the professional being supervised or led is self-motivated, there is no need for an emphasis on task. The supervisory and leadership styles are summarized in Figure 8.2.

Supervisory Style	Leadership Style	Power Base
Directive Control	High-Task/Low-Relationship Dictate/Tell	Position
Directive Informational	Mid-Task/Mid-Relationship Re-Educate	Legal
Collaborative	High-Task/High-Relationship Persuade/Sell	Competence/Respect
Facilitative	Low-Task/High-Relationship Delegate	Person/Charisma

FIGURE 8.2   Situational Leadership Chart

From Glickman, C.D. (1990). *Supervision of Instruction: A Developmental Approach.* Boston: Allyn and Bacon.

From Idol, L., Paolucci-Whitcomb, P., and Nevin, A. (1987). *Collaborative Consultation.* Austin, TX: Pro-Ed.

From Sergiovanni, T.J., and Starratt, R.J. (1979). *Supervision: Human Perspectives.* New York: McGraw-Hill Book Company.

Bases of Power

Although power has been the subject of numerous theorists, conventional conceptualizations of power bases include power of position, power by law, power due to respect/competence, or power based on charisma (Sergiovanni and Starratt, 1979). Leadership power based on position, law, or charisma does not foster metacognitive thinking or reflection on the part of educational collaborators. Individual moral and professional development cannot occur in a system with an inappropriate power base for leadership authority. For optimal collaboration, the preferred power base is respect. True collaboration can occur only when there is respect among the collaborators based on the perceived expertise of each participant. In the consulting model of collaboration, both the consultant and consultee should respect their differing areas of competence. In the coaching model, professionals respect their fellow team member as a competent coach. In the teaming model, each member of the team recognizes and respects the very different areas of expertise of individual team members, from parent to psychologist. Although collaborators may have the power of position or of law, as when the supervisor or organization manager is part of the collaboration, their individual power in the collaborative endeavor comes only with mutual respect for competence and acceptance as a team member.

Preparation for Leadership

Preparing educators for quality leadership in inclusive and collaborative settings involves both content themes and processes (Servatius, Fellows, and Kelly, 1992). Content themes include creating a vision, knowledge of effective instruction, promoting self-direction, building collaboration, facilitating ongoing learning, and dealing with change. Processes that support content include clarifying personal beliefs, encouraging critical self-reflection, exploring alternative perspectives, interning in the schools, practicing intragroup communication facilitation, and role playing in class. Both proposed content themes and proposed learning processes reflect the imperative to appreciate and promote adult development, as well as the appropriate application of leadership for effective collaboration.

Total quality management (TQM), a leadership model for business and industry, has been applied to education and the application has been hotly debated (Bonstingl, 1993; Desjardins and Obara, 1993; Kohn, 1993a, 1993b; Schenkat, 1993; Schmoker and Wilson, 1993). TQM is based on the philosophy of servant leadership, a democratic environment, shared decision making, cooperation, and a climate of trust. A TQM leader emphasizes data gathering to analyze both process and outcome. Under a TQM system, the professional staff collectively use data for making group decisions and for individual self-management. The TQM interaction of systems theory, knowledge, psychology, and variation permits effective resolution of organizational complexity. In educational settings, it facilitates student constructive metacognition, combining new information with previous experience to refine personal meaning. Opposition to TQM arises from the direct application of a business/industrial model to the schools. Unless adapted, the application may not be appropriate. TQM, however, is philosophically compatible with situational leadership theory and supports a school's development into a true learning organization (see Chapter 10).

SUMMARY

This chapter has presented the concepts of adult development and situational leadership. Collaboration often fails due to neglect of these two broad areas. Collaborators must understand and appreciate the different developmental levels or stages of the adults with whom they are working. As educators, we know that meeting children's individual developmental levels will enhance learning. As collaborators, we will have a better chance for successful collaborative interactions if we afford a similar consideration to those individuals with whom we are attempting to collaborate.

Although collaboration connotes professional equity, not all collaborative endeavors are defined by parity. The consulting model involves leadership by the expert. The coaching model involves leadership turn-taking as one or the other collaborators assumes the role of coach. The teaming model, while based on mutual interaction and shared expertise, also entails role release and leadership sharing. Leadership preparation, to be viable, must foster the TQM philosophy of mutual organizational and individual growth. Appropriate application of leadership style will ensure more effective and efficient use of any collaborative model.

VIGNETTE REPRISE

Sarah soon realized that she had to tailor her supervisory style for the individual. With the mature sophomore practicum student, who had years of experience as a classroom assistant, Sarah could be a collaborative supervisor. Together Sarah and the student could decide on practicum goals and attempt to solve class or student problems. With the students for whom this was their first field experience, Sarah employed the directive informational form of supervision.

With two of her junior level field students, Sarah began with a directive informational style but was able to shift gradually to a more collaborative style. Both of the elementary education majors demonstrated growing competence that Sarah supported through collaborative decision making and structured self-reflection on the parts of the students. The English major posed a bit of a problem. Sarah's directive informational style quickly changed to a more controlling style when the student refused to transfer the theories he was learning on campus into classroom practice. Sarah, the methods professors, and the site mentoring teacher met with the student to develop a plan with goals and objectives to be accomplished during the semester so that the English major would not fail his secondary methods class and have to postpone student teaching for a semester.

Sarah's three student teachers posed their own unique challenges. Sarah was able to work in a facilitative style with the double special-general education major. What an experience! Sarah watched the young woman shoulder the full responsibilities of a veteran teacher and accept the role of a professional educator. Her other student teachers were not so successful. By mid semester, one of them realized that she needed to improve in both performance and demeanor. She requested a meeting with Sarah and her site mentor in order to develop an individual growth plan. With continual prompting, oversight, and extended time, she finally earned a passing grade. Even with the direction of a controlling supervisory style, and the support of a conscientious site mentor, Sarah's final student failed the experience. Her failure was as difficult for Sarah and the mentor as it was for the student. In her own evaluation of student teaching, the young woman wrote that after all was said and done, she wished that she had chosen a different major.

PORTFOLIO ACTIVITIES

1. *Personal Application:* Define yourself according to the stages of adult cognitive, moral, and life development, and according to the stages of general and educational career development. (These stages are outlined in Figure 8.1.)

2. *Professional Reflection:* Read the interview with Thomas Sergiovanni in *Educational Leadership* (Brandt, 1992). Do you think that leadership is necessary in professional organizations? Why or why not?

3. *Action Research:* Conduct a leadership survey in your professional organization. Ask the following questions of the administration and of the professional employees.

   - Define leadership.
   - Discuss leadership in terms of situational leadership.
     High-task/low-relationship:
     Mid-task/mid-relationship:

High-task/high-relationship:

Low-task/high-relationship:

- How would you prioritize these leadership styles?

  What is your preferred style of leadership?

  As a leader:

  As a follower:

- Describe the different styles of leadership that you have experienced.

- On the basis of the responses, what hypotheses can you make or what conclusions can you draw?

REFERENCES

Blake, R., and Mouton, J. (1964). *The Managerial Grid.* Houston: Gulf.

Bonstingl, J.J. (1993). "The Quality Movement: What's It Really About?" *Educational Leadership* 51(1): 66.

Brandt, R. (1992). "On Rethinking Leadership: A Conversation with Tom Sergiovanni." *Educational Leadership* 49(5): 46–49.

Burke, P.S., Christensen, J.C., and Fessler, R. (1984). *Teacher Career Stages: Implications for Staff Development.* Bloomington, IN: Phi Delta Kappa Foundation.

Desjardins, C., and Obara, Y. (1993). "From Quebec to Tokyo: Perspectives on TQM." *Educational Leadership* 51(1): 68–72.

Fuller, F.F. (1969). "Concerns of Teachers: A Developmental Conceptualization." *American Educational Research Journal* 6(2): 207–266.

Glickman, C.D. (1990). *Supervision of Instruction,* 2d ed. Boston: Allyn and Bacon.

Glickman, C.D. (1995). *Supervision of Instruction,* 4th ed. Boston: Allyn and Bacon.

Holzman, M. (1992). "Do We Really Need 'Leadership'?" *Educational Leadership* 49(5): 36–40.

Kohlberg, L. (1976). "Moral Stages and Moralization." In T. Lickona (ed.), *Moral Development and Behavior: Theory, Research, and Social Issues.* New York: Holt, Rinehart, and Winston.

Kohlberg, L. (1995). "The Cognitive-Developmental Approach to Moral Education." In A.C. Ornstein and L.S. Behar (eds.), *Contemporary Issues in Curriculum,* 163–175. Boston: Allyn and Bacon.

Kohn, A. (1993). "Reply: The Trouble with Management Models." *Educational Leadership* 51(1): 67.

Kohn, A. (1993). "Turning Learning into a Business: Concerns about Total Quality." *Educational Leadership* 51(1): 58–61.

Morsink, C.V., Thomas, C.C., and Correa, V.I. (1991). *Interactive Teaming: Consultation and Collaboration in Special Programs.* New York: Merrill-Macmillan Publishing Co.

Schenkat, R. (1993). "Deming's Quality: Our Last but Best Hope." *Educational Leadership* 51(1): 64–65.

Schmoker, M., and Wilson, R.B. (1993). "Adapting Total Quality Doesn't Mean 'Turning Learning into a Business'." *Educational Leadership* 51(1): 62–63.

Senge, P.M. (1990). *The Fifth Discipline.* New York: Doubleday/Currency.

Sergiovanni, T.J. (1992). "Why We Should Seek Substitutes for Leadership." *Educational Leadership* 49(5): 41–45.

Sergiovanni, T.J., and Starratt, R.J. (1979). *Supervision: Human Perspectives.* New York: McGraw-Hill Book Company.

Sergiovanni, T.J., Burlingame, M., Coombs, F.S., and Thruston, P.W. (1987). *Educational Governance and Administration,* 2d ed. Englewood Cliffs, NJ: Prentice-Hall, Inc.

Sergiovanni, T.J., Burlingame, M., Coombs, F.S., and Thruston, P.W. (1992). *Educational Governance and Administration,* 3d ed. Englewood Cliffs, NJ: Prentice-Hall, Inc.

Servatius, J.D., Fellows, M., and Kelly, D. (1992). "Preparing Leaders for Inclusive Schools." In R.A. Villa, J.S. Thousand, W. Stainback, and S. Stainback, (eds.), *Restructuring for Caring and Effective Education,* 267–284. Baltimore: Paul H. Brookes Publishing Co.

9

CHANGE IMPLEMENTATION
AND CONFLICT RESOLUTION

Vignette

During the winter holidays, Sarah received a greeting card from a woman she had not heard from in years. Naomi and Sarah had grown up together in a rural western state, but Naomi's father had earned a promotion when the girls were in junior high school, and Naomi's family had relocated to a large metropolitan area in the southwest. Sarah and Naomi had kept in touch throughout high school and college. They had even exchanged visits several times, but as they graduated from school and began their adult lives, they had gradually lost contact. Adult responsibilities had superseded adolescent friendship. Then Sarah received the card. To her delight and amazement, Sarah discovered that Naomi and she still had much in common. The two women began writing regularly and Sarah spent spring break with her friend. Naomi still lived in the town to which her family had moved, now one of the ten largest cities in the country.

Naomi was also in graduate school, working on her doctorate in education. Her dissertation topic was, interestingly enough, collaboration. Naomi's focus was the coaching model. She was working with teachers in several elementary schools in a large suburban school district. The district was wealthy and progressive. The schools were beautiful, relatively new structures. They were built during the open classroom era and had never been redesigned in order to close the classrooms. School faculty worked as grade level teams. There was a fluid feeling in the schools, as teachers and students moved from one area or activity to another. The students were from professionally oriented homes and had the advantages of money, travel, and home-based educational resources. Many students were high achievers who would qualify for traditional accelerated programs, however, the district did not have a specific program for gifted and talented youth. Instead, children were offered the opportunity for pursuing advanced, enriched, or accelerated skills within their daily general education classes. It seemed an anomaly that special education remained a pull-out, service-delivery program.

Naomi had proposed changing this system. She had conducted a series of six training workshops with volunteer general and special education teachers in the fall. The workshops focused on techniques for clinical observation so that the teachers could coach each other in better including special education students in general educational settings. Naomi hypothesized that by training the teachers to observe and coach each other, they would develop more open attitudes toward a reorganization of special education service delivery. If general educators could observe successful instructional techniques used in the resource program with students, and if special educators could observe general education classroom curricula and routines, the teachers would realize how similar their students and educational goals really were. General educators would develop more positive attitudes toward special education students, and special educators would develop more positive attitudes toward collaborating. When Sarah arrived in the spring, she was able to visit the schools with Naomi and conference with the participating teachers. She was able to watch Naomi's coaching project in action.

Sarah discovered that these large, wealthy, suburban schools had educational problems similar to those she had experienced in Blue Spruce. There were at-risk students who did not qualify for needed special education services. There were teachers who were unwilling to collaborate with other teachers and were unwilling to adjust their "standards" to meet individual student needs. Changing business-as-usual in an institution is difficult. Change precipitates conflict. Change requires open minds, continuing administrative support, and the commitment of all involved.

Chapter Outline

Vignette

Chapter Outline

Chapter Content

> *Components of Positive Change Efforts*
> *Decision-Making Strategies for Coping with Change*
>> Step-by-Step Change
> *Cooperative Learning for Conflict Resolution*

Summary

Vignette Reprise

Portfolio Activities

References

COMPONENTS OF POSITIVE CHANGE EFFORTS

Collaboration among educators and between educators and other human services professionals means change for many people. In Chapter 1, we described the traditional view of public education. The individual teacher in the front of a closed classroom, isolated even from the teacher across the hall is passé. Wang, Walberg, and Reynolds (1992) have described the future of special education and in so doing have described changes for general education as well. On the premise that current educational practice relies on complicated bureaucratic procedures, wasted resources, and inefficient use of time, they describe future special education as relying on the following:

- Educational teams
- Effective instructional strategies
- Labeling of programs rather than students
- Individual student progress reports
- Provision for student diversity
- Coordinated teacher preparation
- Coordination among schools, welfare, and health agencies
- Coordination among government offices and programs

The future of public education, if that education is to be effective, will demand change in the form of more coordination and collaboration among all participants.

Neubert and Stover (1994) have suggested that schools for the twenty-first century will encourage collaboration among teachers. Ideal schools in the school reform literature are described with terms such as collegial, collaborative, networking, and teaming. Developing a collaborative school means change from the traditional isolation experienced by teachers in self-contained classrooms. These authors propose that teacher education programs prepare pre-service teachers using the peer coaching model of collaboration. Practice with peer coaching would provide student teachers with experience in one collaborative model and would instill in them an expectation for professional collaboration. What Neubert and Stover suggest is revolutionary change for both pre-service and in-service educators.

Change is not easy to achieve, especially in a bureaucracy. Glickman (1990) discusses the stages of concern with regard to innovation in educational organizations. His conceptualization is based on those of Bents and Howey (1981) and on Hall, Wallace, and Dossett (1973). Stages of concern include:

- Awareness
- Information gathering

- Personalization
- Individual management
- Individual consequences
- Coordination with others
- Refocusing

At the awareness stage, an individual is vaguely aware of an innovation. In order to become better informed, the individual gathers information about the innovation. The individual then personalizes the impending change, considers personal management of the innovation, and ponders consequences to self. The final stages involve collaboration with others in order to coordinate change efforts and personal evaluation of the change with refocusing of personal change implementation.

Key components for successfully implementing educational changes involve support from the institutional leadership, team building among the organization staff, collaboration between the staff and other stakeholders, development of a shared vision, shared planning, a routine system for problem solving, and commitment to the change from all involved. Teachers in one Albuquerque school journaled in order to reflect on their professional growth efforts (Red and Shainline, 1987). Journal reviews produced the following insights into the educational change process:

- Change is a process, not an event.
- Conflict is inevitable and turmoil is unavoidable.
- Change is both personal and complex, but beliefs are mutable.
- Each individual must work out their individual meaning for change and in doing so maintains control of both the appearance and substance of the innovation.

These insights mirror the stages of concern as previously listed. That change is a process becomes evident by an individual's passage from awareness through management to refocusing. Conflict surfaces as the individual attempts personal management of change, realizes its consequences, and coordinates with other individuals also involved in the change. Continual refocusing reflects the journal insight of mutable beliefs. The components for successful change efforts are summarized in Figure 9.1.

Application of components for positive change have reduced resistance to a change in the school counselor's role from that of a direct service provider to that of consultant. Resistance to collaboration in the form of consulting was found to have varied sources (Dougherty, Dougherty, and Purcell, 1991). Teachers may resist collaboration with

---

Involvement *of All Pertinent Stakeholders*

    Administration
    Faculty
    Support Personnel
    Special Services Personnel
    Parents
    Community Agencies
    Local Businesses
    Government Entities

Team Building *among Stakeholders*

    Shared Visioning
    Shared Planning
    Delegated Responsibilities
    System for Problem Management
    Evaluation Plan

Commitment *of All Involved*

    Follow-Through
    Revisions as Needed

Resources *to Support Change*

    Technical Expertise
    Materials and Funding

Leadership *to Maintain Focus*

FIGURE 9.1   Components of Successful Change Efforts

the school counselor due to misconceptions of the counselor's role, a dysfunctional relationship with the counselor, fear of discomfort, fear of disclosing inadequacy, feelings of hopelessness, fear of success, rebellion, or misinterpretation of reality resulting in defensiveness. The resistance can be effectively dealt with using the following strategies reflective of positive change components:

- Maintaining objectivity
- Gaining school support for counselor consulting
- Specifying the counselor's role
- Being cognizant of organizational dynamics
- Using social influence
- Emphasizing the peer nature of the consulting

As special education teachers collaborate with general educators to provide indirect service to students, they encounter the same type of resistance for the same reasons that school counselors have. The strategies listed above for counselors are basically the same as components for successful change in Figure 9.1. The teacher encountering a changing role can maintain objectivity and use social influence by involving all interested stakeholders in planning and implementing the change. Gaining school support, specifying the new role, and maintaining awareness of organizational dynamics flow from team building, with its emphasis on visioning, sharing responsibilities, planning implementation, and evaluating change efforts. Emphasis on the peer nature of the change process can be achieved through stakeholder involvement, team decision making, recognition of the need for external resources and expertise, and respect for necessary but appropriate leadership.

The change of an elementary school from an exclusive to an inclusive philosophy and environment exemplifies components of successful change (Salisbury, Palombaro, and Hollowood, 1993). In a qualitative study, using participant observation, interviews, and school products, researchers discovered:

- Vision-based decisions
- An explicit value base
- An intentional environment
- Professional teaming

Changes that occurred in the school involved changes in structures, policies, pedagogy, and attitudes. The systems change from exclusion to inclusion occurred slowly and intentionally, within a collaborative problem-solving process and with both administrative support and faculty commitment.

Lieberman and McLaughlin (1992) suggested networking as a means of supporting educational change efforts. Effective educational networks share common features. There should be a clear focus for the networking activity. Variety provides participating teachers with flexibility and self-determination. Networking allows for developing discourse communities on any number of educational topics. Teachers who become involved in networking have an increased potential for leadership opportunities by developing expertise in one or several areas. Educational networking supported innovation and change by building a community of teacher-learners.

Finally, Voltz (1993) suggested the following continuum for changing from professional individualism to educational collaboration:

- Routinely exchange student progress information
- Collaboratively develop and coordinate instructional plans
- Pre-teach/post-teach lessons
- Plan for transfer of skills to general education settings
- Provide input into grades and promotion/retention decisions
- Participate in collaborative problem solving
- Direct small group instruction in general education
- Participate in cooperative teaching
- Participate in cooperative professional development

Voltz developed this continuum from less to more collaboration with reference to current school practice. Neither the exchange of student information nor the coordination of instructional plans is innovative. General and special educators regularly cooperate for both purposes. Often special educators pre-teach or post-teach a lesson in the resource room in which the student will also participate while in their mainstream class. Planning for skill transfer may not be as common a practice; usually special educators work on skill transfer without the involvement of general educators. Grading is another area in which one or the other teacher, but not both, make the decisions. Collaborative problem solving usually occurs only during the prereferral process or during IEP meetings. Only with inclusion do special education teachers have the opportunity to co-teach in general education classrooms. Professional development at both the pre-service and in-service levels continues to be separate on most college and university campuses, as well as in the schools. By working through the continuum, educators can start with small changes, make one change at a time, and effect a major restructuring of the educational establishment.

DECISION-MAKING STRATEGIES FOR COPING WITH CHANGE

Conflict is to be expected in any ongoing human interaction, especially if that interaction involves change. A proactive stance with regard to avoiding unnecessary conflict is more productive than a reactive stance of resolution once conflict has erupted. One means of ensuring a positive experience with implementing change is employing a structured method of decision making among the stakeholders in the change effort. Step-by-step decision making allows for individual input and defuses the tension that results from misunderstanding and disempowerment. In this section, several sequential decision-making structures are described. The first, illustrated in Figure 9.2, outlines steps in the change process involving generic considerations for decision making.

Step-by-Step Change

Step 1—visioning. Envision the desired outcome. Each stakeholder in the change process should have the opportunity to share their individual vision for education. Each person's vision deserves the respect and consideration of other group members. Individual visions are combined into the group vision.

Visioning	*Planning and Evaluating*
The Ideal Outcome	An Action Plan
	Responsibilities
Describing	A Calendar
	Formative and Summative Evaluations
The Current Situation	
	Resolving
Listing	
	Vision Commitment
Obstacles	Plan Revisions as Needed
Supports	

FIGURE 9.2   Steps in the Change Process

Step 2—describing. Next describe the current situation. In strategic planning, this step is termed an "environmental scan" and involves brainstorming then listing all components of the current situation whether positive or negative.

Step 3—listing. Following a description of the current situation, obstacles to and supports for the desired outcome can be listed.

Step 4—planning and evaluating. Going beyond description, an action plan is detailed and responsibilities are delegated with specific timelines for completion. Ongoing formative evaluation of change efforts with periodic summative evaluations are essential in determining needed adjustments to the change action plan.

Step 5—resolving. Perhaps the most important step is commitment from all involved to continue to work toward the vision even in the face of obstacles, discouragement, and frustration. "If at first you don't succeed, try, try again!" is a tried and true motto for change efforts.

This generic pattern was specified by Lewin (1951) in his exercise known as force-field analysis. In this process, driving and restraining forces for service delivery are plotted on a force field with the strength of each force estimated. Action choices are made for diminishing or eliminating restraining forces and strengthening or combining driving forces. An action strategy is formulated by answering "who," "what," "where," "how," and "when" questions.

Force-field analysis, as with any productive change, begins with visioning (step 1, previous page). The individual's or organization's goal must be specified. Next, positive and negative forces are listed. The current climate is described in both positive and negative terms (steps 2 and 3, above). The forces are then plotted in a field as shown in Figure 9.3, with restraining (negative) forces plotted against driving (positive) forces of equal strength. After brainstorming ways to diminish restraining forces, and to strengthen driving forces, action steps are outlined (step 4, above).

Force-field analysis is a problem analysis and program implementation technique developed by Kurt Lewin (1951). The process is used for creating resources from service delivery problems and for using all resources as effectively as possible.

1. Identify a goal toward which to strive.
2. List forces driving (+) toward the goal.
3. List forces restraining (–) goal accomplishment.
4. Plot driving (+) and restraining (–) forces on a force field. Indicate strength of each force.

Restraining Forces (–)

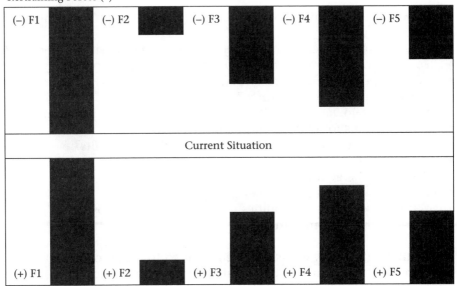

Driving Forces (+)

5. Make an action choice from the following list.
   Brainstorm ways to diminish the strongest restraining (–) forces.
   Brainstorm ways to strengthen the strongest driving (+) forces.
   Eliminate restraining (–) forces.
   Combine driving (+) forces.
   Turn a restraining (–) force into a driving (+) force.
6. Formulate an action strategy.
   List steps for accomplishing the action choice.
   Answer the following questions:
   • *Who* is needed?
   • *What* responsibilities do each of us have?
   • *Where* do we begin?
   • *How* do we begin?
   • *When* will we regroup?

FIGURE 9.3 Force-Field Analysis

From Lewin, K. (1951). *Field Theory in Social Science.* New York: Harper & Row Publishers, Inc. Reprinted with permission.

The force-field action strategy involves assigning personal responsibility for action steps and a schedule for completion (step 4, previous page). With this strategy, a current individual or organizational status quo can be changed in order to reach an improved state of equilibrium.

The collaborative options—outcome planner (COOP) (Welch, Judge, Anderson, Bray, Child, and Franke, 1990) developed for prereferral consultation, can be applied in the change process. The following minor modifications of the COOP questions would make them applicable to systems change.

- How can the situation be described? What are the antecedents and consequences?
- What has been tried for resolving the situation and with what effect?
- For how long has the situation been in its current form?
- What is positive about the situation?
- What would reinforce change?
- Who are involved in the situation, and what is their involvement?
- What options for change can be brainstormed?
- Which options are most likely to achieve desired results?
- What is the specific objective of the chosen option?
- What are the evaluation criteria?
- How and when will progress be measured?
- Who has what responsibilities toward the option chosen?
- When is the next meeting?

As modified, these questions could easily lead to group consensus, provide direction for change efforts, and preclude unnecessary conflict.

Making action plans (MAPS) (Forest and Pearpoint, 1992), described in Chapter 6 as a strategy for IEP development, can be powerful if applied to change decision making. Consider the MAPS questions applied to a school or other human services organization.

- Who is the school?
- What is the school's story?
- What are the school's strengths?
- What are the school's needs?
- What are the school's dreams?
- What are the school's nightmares?
- How do we avoid the nightmares and make the dreams come true?

Just as considerations of these questions can transform the IEP process for an individual student, so can MAPS increase positive communication among professionals and transform the institutional change planning process.

Using a standard group decision-making structure when considering institutional change or educational innovation is a proactive strategy for precluding conflict. However, the nature of change as an unknown, and the tendency of human beings to seek security, make some conflict inevitable. When conflict in group processing does occur, the strategies suggested for cooperative learning among students can be employed for cooperative decision making among adults.

COOPERATIVE LEARNING FOR CONFLICT RESOLUTION

In 1977, shortly after the passage of P.L. 94-142, Arends and Arends projected a change in the role of the school psychologist and wrote a handbook for this changing role. Their projections have proven to be amazingly accurate and the strategies they suggest are pertinent for current educational reform. They suggested that the school psychologist would intervene in education at four levels:

- Direct service to the child
- Indirect service to the child through the teacher
- Direct service to the teacher
- Service to the school system

Arends and Arends insistence on considering "systems" change will be echoed in the final chapter of this book. They emphasize improved communication as a strategy for change and provided the following description of skills pertinent for conflict resolution.

Interpersonal communication can be improved through paraphrasing, describing behavior, describing personal feelings, and checking impressions. In group settings, several task functions will facilitate communication. They include initiating, opinion seeking, clarifying, summarizing, and consensus testing. A seven-step process can facilitate conflict resolution when communication breaks down:

- Equalize motivation of both parties in the conflict
- Equalize the situational power
- Achieve a common definition of the situation
- Define the differences between parties to the conflict
- Provide emotional support to all involved
- Increase the accuracy of communication
- Increase/decrease the sense or urgency to promote an optimal level of tension

Any innovation efforts should strike a balance between being tailored to meet a system's immediate needs and being flexible in order to grow with the system.

Cooperative learning involves change in a smaller system, the classroom, and requires positive communication among students. Johnson and Johnson (Brandt, 1987) list five basic elements for collegiality: group ownership of the outcome, face-to-face interaction, clear individual accountability, social skills, and group debriefing on the cooperative process. These basic components are listed by Thousand and Villa (1990; 1992) as essential for a collaborative professional teaming process.

Positive interdependence means that the group and individual goals are aligned; no one group member is promoting their own hidden agenda. Collaborative social skills for group development include forming (initial trust building), functioning (as a team), formulating (creative problem solving), and fermenting (controversy management). Thousand and Villa suggest a five-step procedure for dysfunctional group behavior:

- Observe the behavior and others' responses
- Attempt to understand the behavior
- Describe the behavior and its impact
- Establish rules for minimizing disruptions
- Turn the unfavorable behavior into a favorable one

They suggest ongoing group processing to promote both positive group functioning and individual accountability. Among the processing techniques are self-reflection, outside observers, audiotaping and/or videotaping, role evaluation, and behavioral goal setting.

Stages of group development as stated by Tuckman (1965; Tuckman and Jensen, 1977) progress from forming through storming, norming and performing. In the forming stage, group members get to know each other. Cummings (1990) suggests several ice breaker activities for groups in the forming stage. One activity is "consensus building" in which group members find five things that all like and five things that they do not like. Another is "I am a person who. . . ." In this activity, each participant describes personal likes, wishes, limitations, and so on. During the storming phase, group members disagree and conflict results. The intensity of this phase can be lessened by assigning a role to each group member. Roles might include the facilitator, recorder, timekeeper, and observer. Group roles should not be static but should be rotated among members at different group meetings. Providing a group with clear directions, or having the group come to consensus with regard to group purpose, will also help the group weather the storming phase. Norming involves setting group rules. An example is allowing only one group member to speak at a time. Finally, a cooperative group can reach the performing phase and accomplish their group task.

The components of cooperative learning echo Arends and Arends's (1977) seven-step process for conflict resolution. Group ownership, face-to-face interaction, and individual accountability address equalization of motivation and situational power of conflicting parties. Social skills, including appropriate verbal and nonverbal communication (see Chapter 3, Figure 3.4 and Figure 3.7), allow for defining differences in an emotionally supportive environment. Tension can be defused through use of cooperative learning strategies.

Educators have been trained to be productive team members (Hammond, Olson, Edson, Greenfield, and Ingalls, 1995). Often teams become dysfunctional due to habits of interaction developed over time, subsystems within the team structure, or team organization. With training, team members develop metacognition of appropriate team functioning and are better able to interact in positive ways. Training of nine teams in three rural regions began with two prerequisites for positive collaboration. Team members shared both ownership of the team goal and interdependence for goal achievement (Burke, 1982). Following prerequisites, team members expected to experience the four stages of team development—forming, storming, norming, and performing (Tuckman, 1965; Tuckman and Jensen, 1977). The seven-step process for team building included identifying a vision, identifying strengths, identifying barriers, setting priorities, identifying roles, identifying team norms, and exploring team member relationships (Beckhard, 1972). Over time and with training as a team, resistance to the process decreased and individual team members developed the ability to discuss intra-team barriers. The resultant team effectiveness permitted the term to challenge system barriers to service delivery for students.

Just as change is not an event but a process, so conflict resolution is an ongoing process. The lack of conflict may indicate a lack of progress. How conflict is supported and resolved is as important as avoiding unnecessary interpersonal misunderstanding. Providing an environment that prevents superfluous conflict while supporting meaningful conflict resolution will allow creative tension to move education or other human services institutions forward in the implementation of innovation.

SUMMARY

Increasing professional collaboration in our bureaucratic educational and human services organizations means a revolutionary change in the ways we normally do business. This chapter has described the components of successful change and has given two examples of change, one in counseling, and the other in education, in which the change components were obvious. Change by its nature involves conflict. Structured decision making was presented as a means of avoiding unnecessary conflict, and cooperative learning strategies were suggested as a means of conflict resolution.

VIGNETTE REPRISE

Sarah knew that more inclusion and collaboration at Blue Spruce School would come only with a price. She would have to expect opposition, resistance, and conflict. Sarah brainstormed proactive strategies for precluding the worst. She felt supported by the fact that student problems and acceptance of innovation were similar regardless of the geographical location, size of the institution, or persons involved. The best beginning, she decided, would be training the school faculty and staff to work as a team, develop a school vision, redefine responsibilities, and change the face of Blue Spruce School through the combined efforts of everyone involved.

PORTFOLIO ACTIVITIES

1. *Personal Application:* Use one or more of the decision-making strategies in your current professional position. Maintain a log of strategies that you apply. Include the following in your log:

   - Describe the strategy.
   - Define your purpose in using the strategy.
   - List supportive elements in your professional environment for the strategy.
   - List obstacles you encountered in strategy implementation.
   - Comment on the success or failure of each strategy application.

2. *Professional Reflection:* Read Chapters 1 and 5 in the 1977 Arends and Arends book on educational systems change. Although written many years ago, how applicable is the information to today's schools? Respond to each part of these two chapters by relating the authors' premises to your professional change efforts.

3. *Action Research:* Summarize your decision-making strategy application log in a chart. Look for underlying themes or relationships.

   - Was strategy success or failure due to inappropriate use?
     To lack of necessary supports?
     To obstacles that were not under your control?

- How could you adapt or modify strategy application in order to better ensure successful implementation?
- Continue implementation, logging, and charting application and your action research.

REFERENCES

Arends, R.I., and Arends, J.H. (1977). *Systems Change Strategies in Educational Settings.* New York: Human Sciences Press.

Beckhard, R. (1972). "Optimizing Team Building Efforts." *Journal of Contemporary Business* 1(3): 23–32.

Bents, R.M., and Howey, K.R. (1981). "Staff Development—A Change in the Individual." *Staff Development/Organization Development: ASCD 1981 Yearbook.* Alexandria, VA: ASCD.

Brandt, R. (1987). "On Cooperation in Schools: A Conversation with David and Roger Johnson." *Educational Leadership* 45(3): 14–19.

Burke, W.W. (1982). *Organizational Development: Principles and Practice.* Boston: Little, Brown and Co.

Cummings, C. (1990). *Managing a Cooperative Classroom.* Edmonds, WA: Teaching, Inc.

Dougherty, A.M., Dougherty, L.P., and Purcell, D. (1991). "The Sources and Management of Resistance to Consultation." *The School Counselor* 38: 178–186.

Forest, M., and Pearpoint, J.C. (1992). "Putting All Kids on the MAP." *Educational Leadership* 50(2): 26–31.

Glickman, C.D. (1990). *Supervision of Instruction.* Boston: Allyn and Bacon.

Hall, G.E., Wallace, R.C., Jr., and Dossett, W.A. (1973). *A Developmental Conceptualization of the Adoption Process within Educational Institutions.* Austin, TX: University of Texas Research and Development Center for Teacher Education.

Hammond, H., Olson, J., Edson, F., Greenfield, R., and Ingalls, L. (1995). "Rural Education Teams: A Team Building Project." *Rural Special Education Quarterly* 14(1): 3–10.

Lewin, K. (1951). *Field Theory in Social Science.* New York: Harper & Row Publishers, Inc.

Lieberman, A., and McLaughlin, M.W. (1992). "Networks for Educational Change: Powerful and Problematic." *Phi Delta Kappan* 73(9): 673–677.

Morsink, C.V., Thomas, C.C., and Correa, V.I. (1991). *Interactive Teaming: Consultation and Collaboration in Special Programs.* New York: Merrill-Macmillan Publishing Co.

Neubert, G.A., and Stover, L.T. (1994). "Peer Coaching in Teacher Education." *Fastback 371.* Bloomington, IN: Phi Delta Kappa Educational Foundation.

Red, C., and Shainline, E. (1987). "Teachers Reflect on Change." *Educational Leadership* 44(5): 38–40.

Salisbury, C.L., Palombaro, M.M., and Hollowood, T.M. (1993). "On the Nature and Change of an Inclusive Elementary School. *JASH* 18(2): 75–84.

Thousand, J.S., and Villa, R.A. (1990). "Sharing Expertise and Responsibilities through Teaching Teams." In W. Stainback and S. Stainback (eds.), *Support Networks for Inclusive Schooling.* Baltimore: Paul H. Brookes Publishing Co.

Thousand, J.S., and Villa, R.A. (1992). "Collaborative Teams: A Powerful Tool in School Restructuring." In R. Villa, J. Thousand, W. Stainback, and S. Stainback (eds.), *Restructuring for Caring and Effective Education.* Baltimore: Paul H. Brookes Publishing Co.

Tuckman, B. (1965). "Developmental Sequence in Small Groups." *Psychological Bulletin* 63: 384–399.

Tuckman, B.W., and Jensen, M.A.C. (1977). "Stages of Small Group Development Revisited." *Group and Organizational Studies* 2: 419–427.

Voltz, D.L. (1993). "Collaboration: Just What Do You Mean, 'Collaborate'?" *L.D. Forum* 17(4): 32–34.

Wang, M.C., Walberg, H., and Reynolds, M.C. (1992). "A Scenario for Better—Not Separate—Special Education." *Educational Leadership* 50(2): 35–38.

Welch, M., Judge, J., Anderson, J., Bray, J., Childs, B., and Franke, L. (1990). "COOP: A Tool for Implementing Prereferral Consultation." *Teaching Exceptional Children* 22(2): 30–31.

10

A SYSTEMS PERSPECTIVE ON *MODELS OF COLLABORATION*

Vignette

As Sarah made the final revisions on her thesis and prepared for its defense, she contemplated the next few months. She hated to leave the university environment. The intellectual excitement of classes and the currency of thought would not be continued with the same intensity back on the high line. The close friendships engendered by living together, lunchtime debates in the student cafeteria, after-class gatherings at a local coffee house, and surviving the constant pressures and tensions of graduate study could not be duplicated. On the other hand, Sarah was excited to put her new-found knowledge to the test in Blue Spruce.

Sarah knew that she would be expected to share what she had learned. She was not sure how comfortable she would be with collaborating in the consulting model. Sarah did not view herself as an "expert" in any area. The principal, however, had already contacted her with regard to developing sessions for the traditional August in-service days at the beginning of the school year. He wanted Sarah to inform the school staff about the latest federal and state special education regulations. Because she had applied for and been granted a second sabbatical year in order to complete her thesis, Sarah felt obligated to comply with his request. She guessed that she would be using consulting for the purpose of technical assistance.

She planned to begin clinical observation cycles with three teachers with whom she worked well. They taught at different levels in the school; one was the kindergarten teacher, the second was being administratively transferred from first to fifth grade in the coming school year, and the third taught art in high school. Sarah hoped that these would be collaborative efforts in the coaching model and that the coaching would support inclusive educational practice, at least in these three instances. The purpose of coaching would be collegial support, an important factor as the four of them worked through individual student inclusion issues.

Sarah began imagining all the creative ways that Blue Spruce School could be changed for the better. She knew that "change" in a small-town school with a conservative philosophy was considered a bad word, but she dreamed anyway. She thought about Naomi. Naomi worked with a small team of teachers in a few schools in her large suburban Texas school district. With administrative support, Naomi's dissertation project was spreading district-wide. Perhaps if Sarah pulled together a group of interested school and community people, she could begin an incremental change effort using the teaming model of collaboration. The purpose of this teaming would be long-term goal setting and solving immediate challenges to goal attainment.

Sarah recognized the impact that adult and career development would have on her efforts. In the two years that she had been away, Blue Spruce had hired several new teachers. Several others were coasting until their retirement. She could name one or two rather young teachers who applied for positions elsewhere every year because they felt personally isolated and professionally frustrated in a community and school the size of Blue Spruce. She wondered why they stayed on. She would have to master the art of situational leadership in order to work optimally with such adult diversity.

Finally, Sarah thought about Blue Spruce as a learning organization. She hoped that she could be instrumental in promoting integration of all the systems impacting education in her home community. What did Senge's (1990) archetypes have to say for the Blue Spruce School and how could it become a place where both institutional and personal growth were valued and promoted? Sarah was as excited to meet the challenges facing her as she was reluctant to end her master's sojourn.

Chapter Outline

Vignette

Chapter Outline

Chapter Content

      Review of Previous Chapters
      Context of Collaboration
            Societal Diversity
            Schools as Learning Organizations
            School Renewal

Summary

Portfolio Activities

References

REVIEW OF PREVIOUS CHAPTERS

The purpose of this book has been to provide a structure for collaborative practice. As society changes, the student population diversifies, and inclusive educational practice becomes the norm, collaboration among educators and between education and other human services becomes imperative. Although the literature on collaboration is increasing, no where has the bigger picture been addressed. Bits and pieces of the collaboration puzzle have been discussed, but there has been no understanding of the collaborative gestalt. This book presents such an overview for collaborative practice. It provides models of collaboration—consulting, coaching, and teaming—that can be employed along with a rationale for appropriate use in Chapters 4, 5, and 6. With this information, collaborators can analyze a particular situation, choose the best model for the situation, and evaluate the effectiveness of their collaborative practice. In addition, this book presents three overriding purposes for collaboration—technical assistance, collegial support, and challenge solutions (Garmston, 1987) that are discussed in Chapter 7.

Legal support for collaborative practice is explored in Chapter 2. The framers of the original special education legislation, the Education of the Handicapped Act, passed in 1975, mandated that students with disabilities be educated in the least restrictive environment (LRE) possible. Both court rulings, as well as subsequent reauthorizations of the law have supported the LRE concept and a team approach to educational programming.

Other factors relevant to effective collaborative practice have been explored in various chapters of the book. Clinical observation is discussed in Chapter 3 as a basic tool for collaborative practice. Through systematic and ongoing observation, collaborators can collect objective evidence for solving educational dilemmas and supporting each other in individual professional growth. The impact of adult development and the importance of appropriate leadership for effective collaboration are presented in Chapter 8. In Chapter 9, collaboration is viewed as educational change and considerations for any institutional change effort are presented. Effective communication skills and ways to deal with conflict are essential in any collaborative effort. Communication, addressed in Chapter 3, is revisited in Chapter 9 with relation to conflict prevention and resolution.

Collaboration is often discussed in isolation, and the skills facilitating collaborative practice are developed discretely. Factors supporting the larger structure of collaboration and factors impacting collaborative practice combine to form essential elements for effective implementation of collaboration in education and across the human services. Previous chapters provide models of collaboration, along with internal factors to be considered when collaborating. This chapter provides an external context for collaborative practice.

CONTEXT OF COLLABORATION

Societal Diversity

That the student population is changing seems to be commonly accepted. Family diversity has become the norm, rather than the exception. The definition of "family" has changed over the past forty years from father, mother, Dick, and Jane to various configurations. There are single parent families, reconstructed families with father, mother, yours, mine, and our children, foster families of more or less permanence, and the extended families of various ethnic groups. As a teacher, it is easy to make a mistake and call one or the other parent by the wrong last name. Surrogate parents must sometimes be designated by the court system in order to have a child advocate at school-related meetings and in order to procure legally defensible signatures for service delivery.

Diversity in student ability is increasingly recognized. In the school population, while students with disabilities have been the subject of collaboration for over twenty years, other subsets of the student body cannot be overlooked. Students with a disability as defined by Section 504, who do not qualify for special education services, require a group effort for educational planning. Programs for children with exceptional talent in some area go through extensive screening in most school districts in order to participate in extended studies. Such screening and subsequent programming cannot be accomplished without the combined efforts of many different individuals. The "average" students, who do not qualify for any specialized service delivery, exhibit a wide range of abilities and talents. An individual teacher, working alone, is hard pressed to meet the needs of each "average" learner, let alone accommodate a broader definition of student diversity.

Diversity in gender must be addressed. Issues of sexual discrimination and harassment must be continually allayed by professionals in education and the human services. Old beliefs about the superiority of one sex or the other in different subject areas cannot be tolerated. Teachers must constantly be on the alert to pay equal attention to, ask similar questions of, and address behavioral issues similarly with both male and female students. Career exploration and professional encouragement should be directed similarly for students of both sexes.

The tremendous diversity in American subcultures must be embraced. Mere tolerance of ethnic diversity is not acceptable. To embrace our differences is to promote their enrichment of American society. Rather than not recognizing holidays in order to avoid offending individuals, why not study everyone's holidays? Developing an understanding of different beliefs and customs is educationally sound and personally enriching. Celebration of our cultural differences allows discovery of our human similarities.

Provision of an optimal education for each student cannot be the responsibility of one teacher. From the perspective of education as part of the larger societal system, the educational implications are individually overwhelming. No one person can know everything, be involved everywhere, and be all things to all students. The complexity of current society demands collaboration. From a legal perspective, collaboration is mandated, either directly or indirectly, by legislation reinforced by case law. From a perspective of change, collaboration is a change in the way educational organizations function and, as such, demands administrative support and team commitment. A school as only one subsystem of the larger society must synchronize with the other subsystems in mutual collaboration in order for individuals to be effective.

Schools as Learning Organizations

Peter Senge has produced a thought provoking book entitled *The Fifth Discipline* (1990). He describes business and industry as learning organizations. Senge expands systems theory into five disciplines, the fifth of which is "Team Learning." Leading to Team Learning are the disciplines of Systems Thinking, Personal Mastery, Mental Models, and Building Shared Vision. Each discipline can be thought of in terms of practices, principles, and essences. Practices are what practitioners do; practices are the focus of time and energy.

Underlying the practices are principles—the theories of each discipline. Learning combines theory and practice; learning means both new understandings and new behaviors. Essences of the disciplines are a state of being experienced only with discipline mastery. The five disciplines—Systems Thinking, Personal Mastery, Mental Models, Building Shared Vision, and Team Learning—have been outlined in Figure 10.1.

Senge describes ten systems archetypes that he ascribes to business or industry systems, but each applies to education and to other human services, as well. The first is "Balancing Process with Delay." This structure involves an organization with a goal overreacting to delayed feedback. An educational example of this structure is a district responding to quick but unsustained student population growth by building new facilities that shortly become ghost schools. This often occurs in rural

Systems Thinking	Practices	Simulation
		System Archetypes
	Principles	Leverage
		Policy Resistance
		Structure Influences Behavior
	Essences	Interconnectedness
		Holism
Personal Mastery	Practices	Making Choices
		Creative Tension
		Personal Vision
	Principles	Subconscious
		Creative v. Emotional Tension
		Vision
	Essences	Connectedness
		Generativeness
		Being
Mental Models	Practices	Left-Hand Column
		Testing Assumptions
		Distinguishing Data from Abstractions
	Principles	Balance Inquiry and Advocacy
		Ladder of Inference
		Espoused Theory v. Theory-in-Use
	Essences	Openness
		Love of Truth
Building Shared Vision	Practices	Acknowledging Current Reality
		Visioning Process
	Principles	Commitment v. Compliance
		Shared Vision as Hologram
	Essences	Partnership
		Commonality of Purpose
Team Learning	Practices	Practicing
		Surfacing Own Defensiveness
		Acting as Colleagues
		Suspending Assumptions
	Principles	Defensive Routines
		Integrate Dialogue and Discussion
		Dia Logos
	Essences	Alignment
		Collective Intelligence

FIGURE 10.1 Senge's Learning Disciplines

From *The Fifth Discipline* by Peter M. Senge. Copyright © 1990 by Peter M. Senge. Used by permission of Doubleday, a division of Bantam Doubleday Dell Publishing Group, Inc.

areas with mine development. When the mine is no longer functioning, the mining company moves out and the area is left with unneeded school structures. A similar phenomenon occurs in large urban areas when the city expands rapidly then experiences a period of economic recession and decline.

The second systems archetype is "Limits to Growth." Growth in any system is response to reinforcing feedback processes. Eventually growth slows and collapse accelerates. An educational example of this is early special education referral of students with suspected learning disabilities. Because there was federal money to be had by student identification, schools liberally interpreted LD qualifying standards and over-identified students as needing special education under this category. As the reinforcing dollars dwindled, schools became more conservative in their identification procedures. Providing the needed services without the necessary monetary resources accelerated collapse of quality special education services.

"Shifting the Burden," the third archetype, occurs when a short-term solution is used to correct a problem. Although short-term benefit may accrue, the long-term repercussions may adversely affect the organization. An educational example is improper understanding and implementation of "inclusion" in order to save money. Placing students with special educational needs in general education classrooms without the necessary resources and supports will result in immediate dollar savings, but long-term negative repercussions in the quality of education for all students.

"The Special Case: Shifting the Burden to the Intervenor," archetype four, occurs when intervenors try to solve problems. The special education classroom assistant who accompanies a student with disabilities to the general education classroom, hovers over the student, and works strictly one-on-one with them, actually encourages learned dependence and helplessness. The burden of learning independence for community inclusion is stifled by the well-meaning "intervenor."

"Eroding Goals," archetype five, seems to be a perennial problem in institutions of higher education in the form of grade inflation. With increasing enrollment due to societal expectations of higher education degrees, the quality of students may decline. In college and university graduate programs, however, students maintain expectations of accomplishing "A" work in their graduate studies. The result can be a gradual decline in institutional requirements, with institutional acceptance of less than optimal student performance.

A similar phenomenon occurs in low socioeconomic school environments. As students come to school unprepared for traditional mainstream expectations, school personnel gradually dilute their requirements. The result is ongoing erosion of educational standards in some schools. As this occurs, the gap in expectations between wealthy schools with high standards and schools operating from a lower tax base, often in minority neighborhoods, increases. Over time, the increasing division between classes will mean the loss of potential talent at great cost to American society.

The sixth archetype is "Escalation," exemplified by educational institutions fighting for dwindling state and federal funding. The ensuing political battles result in the buildup of misunderstanding, miscommunication, and competition between institutions, rather than the cooperative behavior that could benefit all students.

Two entities competing for limited support or resources with one gaining and the other starving defines the seventh archetype, "Success to the Successful." For the past twenty years, educational programs for students who are at risk or who have disabilities have been thriving while programs for students with exceptional abilities have declined due to lack of necessary resources.

When individuals use a commonly available but limited resource until the resource is significantly depleted, the "Tragedy of the Commons," archetype eight, occurs. An individual school has a fixed duplication budget for the year. Teacher A is compulsive and organized; she plans her monthly units and daily lessons well in advance and has the district print shop duplicate the needed worksheets. So thoroughly has she planned that she has a year's worth of duplication completed by the end of the first quarter. Teacher B, on the other hand is spontaneous. In May, his students decide during a class meeting to begin studying dinosaurs because they can visit nearby tracks that have been buried in snow all winter. Teacher B requests duplication of a map of the track area, and pictures of the tracks to aid student field identification. Unfortunately, there is no budget left in order to honor his request and the students are left with no self-directed materials during their field experience.

The ninth archetype, "Fixes that Fail," has been traditional in special education. Skill drills focusing on phonics, math facts, or spelling words have been the educational practice of choice for years. It was reasoned that students needed these prerequisites before applying the skills to problem solving or using them in conceptually more complex activities. Quite frequently, although a student may have problems with the "basics," if given the chance, they may be creative problem solvers and capable of complex higher-order thinking tasks.

The tenth and final system archetype described by Senge is "Growth and Underinvestment." This archetype occurs repeatedly as needed funding for education is cut and cut again by state legislatures and the federal government. Educators work with the future; students today will be the productive citizens of tomorrow. As funding is cut for necessary educational programs, performance standards of schools decline and a vicious cycle begins. Legislators try to counter this decline by mandating increasingly stringent educational requirements. For schools to improve, however, they need resources, not guidelines. The guidelines will come from

I. Balancing Process with Delay

II. Limits to Growth

III. Shifting the Burden

IV. Special Case: Shifting the Burden to the Intervenor

V. Eroding Goals

VI. Escalation

VII. Success to the Successful

VIII. Tragedy of the Commons

IX. Fixes That Fail

X. Growth and Underinvestment

FIGURE 10.2 Senge's Systems Archetypes

From *The Fifth Discipline* by Peter M. Senge. Copyright © 1990 by Peter M. Senge. Used by permission of Doubleday, a division of Bantam Doubleday Dell Publishing Group, Inc.

the visioning and teamwork in a learning organization. Cuts in funding result in minimal growth because of underinvestment (Figure 10.2).

As educators master the five learning disciplines and schools become learning organizations, understanding of the systems archetypes is essential. Visions that are either created individually or shared in the spirit of team learning will focus on one or more of the archetypes. To master the five disciplines, an organization may employ all of the collaborative models.

At first, the organization may call on an outside consultant for initial training and to serve as a change agent. The consultant may work with a school for a year or more providing new information to the school administration, faculty, and staff. Not only would the staff read *The Fifth Discipline,* but they would gain an understanding of how they as individuals could master the disciplines, and how their school, as a whole, could grow into a learning organization The consultant would also teach the school personnel to recognize and counter the systems archetypes through lecture, discussion, and case-study activities.

After gaining the necessary basic information, members of the organization may coach each other toward discipline mastery. In dyads, the school personnel could help each other to understand the principles and to work through practices in order to achieve mastery and experience the essence of each of the five disciplines. Because this is an ongoing process, the coaching dyads may need the continuing support and guidance of a consultant. Following the year of initial training, the consultant should be available to provide ongoing technical assistance and expertise as dyads struggle to gain discipline mastery.

Finally, Team Learning, the fifth discipline, will allow educational and other human services organizations both to maintain vision and to constructively work through solutions to archetypal situations. Team Learning is the epitome of the Teaming Model of collaboration. Team Learning recognizes that each individual's personal agenda is important for maintaining organizational health. Team Learning incorporates the concept of role release as team members accept and relinquish the varied roles necessary for effective team functioning. Team Learning accepts conflict as a positive aspect of the change needed for educational progress. In understanding the worth of conflict, members of a learning team are able to objectify conflicting opinions, enter into professional dialogue, and resolve the issues. Team Learning uses the Teaming Model of collaboration to promote philosophical diversity while facilitating consensus building in the environment of a learning organization.

Although Senge has written for a business community, his concepts readily apply to educational institutions. At the same time, there has been a growing body of literature addressing school reform, restructuring, and renewal. This parallel body of literature is compatible with the concept of the learning organization and has begun to incorporate Senge's work.

School Renewal

Current literature addressing school renewal efforts seems to assume collaboration and echoes other chapter themes in this book. Themes of educational renewal include collaboration, ongoing professional development, supportive leadership, continuing change, and a systems perspective.

Collaboration, the first theme in renewal, is usually described as teamwork. In comparing schools to adapting organisms, Garmston and Wellman (1995) stress "interdependence" as the connecting element and as necessary if the school is to adapt. Wagner (1993) calls for focus group sessions and town meetings where groups with differing opinions as to the purpose of education can come to common understandings.

Evans (1993) stresses the need for staff to work together, for participation in collaborative decision making, and for clear communication at all levels. Joyce and Calhoun (1995) suggest that by working in small groups, faculty can become nurturants for one another.

In fact, collaboration for school renewal goes beyond personnel to involve students and the community. Managing classrooms by committees (Blythe and Bradbury, 1993), organizing schools into small units as an alternative to tracking (Oxley, 1994), and establishing persistent student groups to overcome the gang mentality and promote learning (Wynne and Walberg, 1994), have been positive student collaborative strategies toward school improvement. Collaboration between school and community has been described by DeBevoise (1986) and by Stone (1995). DeBevoise described successful collaboration between universities and schools based on administrative support, voluntary involvement, realistic expectations, consumer satisfaction, effective service delivery, and noninvolvement with the alter institution's internal politics. Stone suggested that school–community collaboration exists at three levels— between executives, among professionals, and with parents. For educational institutions to renew themselves, both intraschool and inter-school–community collaboration are essential.

Ongoing development is the second theme in educational reform. Tewell (1995) states that one approach for supporting central office administrators through school restructuring is providing opportunities for learning. Joyce and Calhoun (1995) suggest connecting faculty to the knowledge base on teaching and learning then structuring the school to provide time for collective inquiry. Senge's (1990) concept of team learning is the goal in any learning organization where individuals and organization continue to develop and grow through mutual dependence. Schools should be learning organizations for the teachers, as well as the students (O'Neil, 1995). Child-centered education at Beacon Hill School (Roesener, 1995), brain-based learning at Dry Creek Elementary School (Caine and Caine, 1995), transformation of tracking to create achievers at Adlai E. Stevenson High School (DuFour, 1995), and students questioning the school structure at South Brunswick High School (Lott, 1995), all exemplify ongoing learning throughout the school and community populations. Renewal means a never ending quest for knowledge. Such renewal calls for collaboration throughout the organization and application of the consulting, coaching, and teaming models.

A third theme in educational reform literature is appropriate and effective leadership. Decision-making authority should shift to the persons affected by the decisions (Garmston and Wellman, 1995). For this to happen, the governance system has to be restructured to allow for a consensual process (O'Neil, 1993a). Evans (1993) calls for "authentic" leaders who motivate their followers because of their own credibility. Reitzug and Burrello (1995) list three types of behaviors through which principals can build self-renewing schools:

- Providing a supportive environment for examining and reflecting on practice
- Using behaviors such as asking questions, wandering around the school, and challenging practice
- Making implementation of promising ideas possible

Appropriate leadership such as total quality management (see Chapter 8, section: "Preparation for Leadership") can facilitate concomitant individual and organizational growth resulting in educational renewal. Application of appropriate leadership is one method of supporting collaboration and is an essential ingredient of reform.

Educational reform/restructuring/renewal means change, the fourth theme. Change is sometimes unnoticeable, sometimes revolutionary. Renewal of the educational organization cannot occur without openness and commitment to the change. Garmston and Wellman (1995) talk about the need for schools to be adaptive organizations. Tewell (1995) cautions that without the necessary supports in place, change can result in psychological fallout and staff paralysis. Evans (1993) describes change as bereavement. He counsels change agents to be aware of and to support the human factor through the grieving process. Anderson (1993) lists stages—awareness, exploration, transition, emergence, and predominance—and elements—vision, public support, networking, teaching/learning, and administrative responsibilities—of change. She provides a matrix for managing the components of change efforts by developing a common language among diverse groups, developing a plan for moving forward systematically, and developing ongoing assessment of quality. That change should be never ending is emphasized by Sagor (1995) who describes the "It" syndrome. Reform movements often claim to have "the answer" and educators tend to look for "the strategy." Sagor maintains that chances are today's "It" won't be tomorrow's. Joyce and Calhoun (1995) repeat this in terms of change as inquiry rather than formula. Any school reform effort will fail, and many have, in the absence of a supportive environment, open minds, and individual commitment to the change. Committed collaboration among all stakeholders is the sine qua non of the change process.

Senge points out that fragmenting pervades educational institutions; innovation has been by the individual teacher in an individual classroom (O'Neil, 1995). The first discipline to be mastered if an organization is to thrive is systems thinking which constitutes the fifth theme pervading educational renewal efforts. Holzman (1993) defines systemic change with the following indicators:

- Systemic change involves the school system from district to state.
- Systemic change involves every unit in the system.
- Systemic change includes every aspect of the system.
- Systemic change should be systematic.
- Systemic change is fundamental, not superficial change.

Smith points out that systemic reform is a long-term struggle, and reform success depends upon less centralized control and more support for local initiative (O'Neil, 1993b). Wagner (1993) poses the following five questions to be answered for system change. These questions closely parallel those posed by Lewin (1951) forty years ago in the force-field analysis for problem solving in program implementation. (See Chapter 9, section: "Step-by-Step Change.")

- What are the school's strengths and weaknesses?
- What are the school's vision and core values?
- What are priorities and strategies?
- What structures are needed?
- What new skills and resources are needed?

Collaboration is both a component of and a support for current educational renewal efforts. The models of collaboration—consulting, coaching, and teaming—apply to and occur in the systems context of increasing societal diversity and of schools as learning organizations.

SUMMARY

This chapter has provided a context for *Models of Collaboration.* It began with a review of previous chapters that have provided both a structure for collaborative practice in the form of collaboration models, as well as an exploration of factors impacting collaborative practice. The chapter concluded with the current external contexts for collaboration. These contexts include the need to embrace student diversity in all its forms for the enrichment of our society, consideration of education and human services institutions as learning organizations, and the continuing pursuit of renewal as educational institutions restructure. Collaboration, the working together toward a common end, emerges as an imperative within educational institutions, between education and other human services agencies, and across societal systems.

PORTFOLIO ACTIVITIES

In order to complete the following activities, it may be helpful to refer to *The Fifth Discipline* (Senge, 1990).

1. *Personal Application:* Use specific examples from the professional organization in which you work for each of Senge's systems archetypes.

   - Balancing Process with Delay
   - Limits to Growth
   - Shifting the Burden
   - Special Case: Shifting the Burden to the Intervenor
   - Eroding Goals
   - Escalation
   - Success to the Successful
   - Tragedy of the Commons
   - Fixes that Fail
   - Growth and Under Investment

2. *Professional Reflection:* Evaluate the professional organization in which you work in terms of practices, principles, and essences in each of Senge's five learning disciplines.

   - Systems Thinking
   - Personal Mastery
   - Mental Models
   - Building Shared Vision
   - Team Learning

3. *Action Research:* Make an action plan for developing one of the learning disciplines in your current professional position.

   - Use the evaluation completed in number 2 above to determine on which discipline it is that you are going to focus.
   - Plan a strategy(ies) for development of practices, or principles, and essences in that discipline.
   - Implement your plan for one area (practices, or principles, or essences).
   - Evaluate your implementation and suggest your next step.

REFERENCES

Anderson, B.L. (1993). "The Stages of Systemic Change." *Educational Leadership* 51(1): 14–17.

Blythe, M.C., and Bradbury, P.M. (1993). "Classroom by Committee." *Educational Leadership* 50(7): 56–58.

Caine, R.N., and Caine, G. (1995). "Reinventing Schools through Brain-Based Learning." *Educational Leadership* 52(7): 43–47.

DeBevoise, W. (1986). "Collaboration: Some Principles of Bridgework." *Educational Leadership* 43(5): 9–12.

DuFour, R. (1995). "Restructuring Is Not Enough." *Educational Leadership* 52(7): 33–37.

Education of All Handicapped Children Act of 1975. P.L. 94-142. U.S.C. §1401 (1975).

Evans, R. (1993). "The Human Face of Reform." *Educational Leadership* 51(1): 19–23.

Garmston, R.J. (1987). "How Administrators Support Peer Coaching." *Educational Leadership* 49(5): 18–26.

Garmston, R., and Wellman, B. (1995). "Adaptive Schools in a Quantum Universe." *Educational Leadership* 52(7): 6–13.

Holzman, M. (1993). "What Is Systemic Change?" *Educational Leadership* 51(1): 18.

Joyce, B., and Calhoun, E. (1995). "School Renewal: An Inquiry, Not a Formula." *Educational Leadership* 52(7): 51–55.

Lewin, K. (1951). *Field Theory in Social Science.* New York: Harper & Row Publishers, Inc.

Lott, J.G. (1995). "When Kids Dare to Question Their Education." *Educational Leadership* 52(7): 38–52.

O'Neil, J. (1993). "On Systemic Reform: A Conversation with Marshall Smith." *Educational Leadership* 51(1): 12–13.

O'Neil, J. (1993). "Turning the System on Its Head." *Educational Leadership* 51(1): 8–11.

O'Neil, J. (1995). "On Schools as Learning Organizations: A Conversation with Peter Senge." *Educational Leadership* 52(7): 20–23.

Oxley, D. (1994). "Organizing Schools into Small Units: Alternatives to Homogeneous Grouping." *Phi Delta Kappan* 75(7): 521–526.

Reitzug, U.C., and Burrello, L.C. (1995). "How Principals Can Build Self-Renewing Schools." *Educational Leadership* 52(7): 48–50.

Roesener, L. (1995). "Changing the Culture at Beacon Hill." *Educational Leadership* 52(7): 28–32.

Sagor, R. (1995). "Overcoming the One-Solution Syndrome." *Educational Leadership* 52(7): 24–27.

Senge, P.M. (1990). *The Fifth Discipline.* New York: Doubleday/Currency.

Stone, C.R. (1995). "School/Community Collaboration." *Phi Delta Kappan* 76(10): 794–800.

Tewel, K.J. (1995). "Despair at the Central Office." *Educational Leadership* 52(7): 65–68.

Wagner, T. (1993). "Systemic Change: Rethinking the Purpose of School." *Educational Leadership* 51(1): 24–29.

Wynne, E.A., and Walberg, H.J. (1994). "Persisting Groups: An Overlooked Force for Learning." *Phi Delta Kappan* 75(7): 527–530.

APPENDIX

PATTERN ANALYSIS

1. Teacher: All of us are finished. OK. Close your books. Now mainly the recorders will be the ones talking right now. If there's anybody in the group needing to add something, feel free to raise your hands. OK? Your first question was, "How were the homes in Tenochtitlan similar to the homes in Houston? Would anybody like to talk about that? Erin?

2. Student: (Indecipherable)

3. Teacher: OK. Do we have that? Now, that's how the houses were in Tenochtitlan. Do we have homes like that in Houston? What (name)?

4. Student: (Indecipherable)

5. Teacher: We have stone houses. That's correct. Do we have homes that are stucco?

6. Student: (Indecipherable)

7. Teacher: They do. They do. They use stucco. Mostly for decoration, but they use stucco. OK. Does anyone . . . (calls on student)?

8. Student: Our homes are still made of stucco (Indecipherable).

9. Teacher: OK, some houses are better than others. OK. You mean as far as quality goes?

10. Student: (Indecipherable)

11. Teacher: OK. This is true. Can you elaborate a little more on that? Can you explain what you mean?

12. Student: (Indecipherable)

13. Teacher: We have single houses. Some of the houses, if you will remember, that we read about in Tenochtitlan . . . Some of

the homes. . . . It talked about going from the outside of the city to the inside, to the heart of the city, and it said as you . . . The homes on the outside were of poorer quality. They weren't as nice as the ones in closer to town. Now we might not have the same arrangement in Houston. The houses on the outside might be nicer than the houses in the heart of the city. Still, we do have the mixture. Some houses are of poorer quality; some are of better quality. OK. Would anyone else like to add anything? (Calls on student.)

14. Student: (Indecipherable)
15. Teacher: OK. They are crowded together. That's a good point. Are the homes in Houston crowded together?
16. Student: (Indecipherable)
17. Teacher: Some more than others, but very few houses cover what I would say, a lot of land. Houses have very small patches of land. Pam?
18. Student: (Indecipherable)
19. Teacher: Many of them, she said, were made of adobe and bricks. We use bricks here, not the same type, but we use bricks. So, many of the homes are made of the same materials back then as now. Would anyone like to add anything else? (Waits for reply.) Let's go on to number two. "What would a shopping area in Houston have in common with the marketplace in Tenochtitlan?" There's a big description about the marketplace in Tenochtitlan in your book. Theresa, what do y'all have?
20. Student: (Indecipherable)
21. Teacher: That's correct. They both sell things. Maybe not the same type. Maybe they didn't use dollars and quarters, but they used some form of money. They used. . . . What did they use? Do you remember?
22. Student: (Indecipherable)
23. Teacher: Cacao beans.
24. Student: (Indecipherable)
25. Teacher: They were both crowded. They both sold similar things. Can you be a little more specific about the kinds of things?
26. Student: (Indecipherable)
27. Teacher: (Repeats, but still indecipherable)
28. Student: Both places sold food. Both places (indecipherable). Both places sold juniper.
29. Teacher: Everyone needs to be listening to what everyone says. Pam?
30. Student: (Indecipherable)

31. Teacher: They were both busy. They were both crowded. I know how Sharpstown Mall gets. It's so crowded, I don't even like to go there, sometimes it's so crowded. Erin?
32. Student: (Indecipherable)
33. Student: (Indecipherable)
34. Teacher: Thank you, that's a good point. They had some kind of security in their marketplaces. We also have a type of security. Maybe they have a security guard. Many of our malls. . . . Even grocery stores have some type of security. So, both marketplaces have security of some form. That's a very good point. OK. Is there anything you would like to add? Would you like to add anything? Remember, now, if you want to add anything and you're not necessarily the reporter, feel free to raise your hand. OK. Number three. "How is Houston's method of supplying water similar to that of Tenochtitlan?" Roxanne, did you have your hand up? Do you want to give your answer? Did you have an answer?
35. Student: (Indecipherable)
36. Teacher: They have sewer problems. Do we have sewer problems here?
37. Student: Yes!
38. Teacher: OK. Do y'all have anything else down?
39. Student: Where did they get their water?
40. Teacher: From lakes. Remember, it was built on a lake? In the beginning, they used spring water from springs. We use water from manmade lakes and reservoirs. Anything else?
41. Student: (Something about aqueducts)
42. Teacher: Yeah. OK. Do we have anything similar today in Houston?
43. Student: Canals.
44. Teacher: OK. First, tell me what is a canal? Can anybody tell me what is a canal? David?
45. Student: (Indecipherable)
46. Teacher: No. You're thinking about a dike. That's a dike. A canal is a manmade waterway. Can anyone think of any canals that we might have in Houston? Romeo?
47. Student: (Indecipherable)
48. Teacher: Bayous? What?
49. Student: (Indecipherable)
50. Teacher: Braes Bayou. Now, it may not be manmade, but very often, the bayous are improved. They build up the sides with cement and clean them up. Things like that. (Calls on student.)

51. Student: (Indecipherable)
52. Teacher: OK. They both supply a need. They are supplying the water. We both have pipes. What did the Aztecs use? There's something that carries water, manmade . . . ? Ruby?
53. Student: Aqueducts.
54. Teacher: Aqueducts. Here we use our bayous and ditches for carrying the water, but we have a system of pipes which carry water all over the city of Houston. Erin?
55. Student: (Indecipherable) (something about water)
56. Teacher: They both emptied water into . . . ?
57. Student: (Indecipherable)
58. Teacher: OK. That's correct. Tenochtitlan had a lake that they emptied their water into. We have lakes around here. We have the gulf nearby that our water is emptied into. George?
59. Student: (Indecipherable)
60. Teacher: They both had problems supplying water to the town. That's correct. They both had a problem.
61. Student: (Indecipherable)
62. Teacher: Oh, that was for number four. Yeah, number three.
63. Student: (Indecipherable)
64. Teacher: They had a reservoir and they used spring water, Tenochtitlan, in the beginning. But as the city got real crowded, they had to think of something else, but in the beginning, they used spring water. OK. Let's go on to number four. Do they share anything, our sanitation and Tenochtitlan? Erin?
65. Student: (Indecipherable)
66. Teacher: OK. There were people who took care of getting rid of garbage. Theresa?
67. Student: (Indecipherable)
68. Teacher: They had garbage men. Romeo, you need to pay attention.
69. Student: (Indecipherable)
70. Teacher: They even, they had street sweepers. Has anybody here seen the street sweepers in Houston?
71. Student: Yeah, oh yeah!
72. Student: They go down the street and they're really loud.
73. Teacher: They're very loud. They're great big machines. Now in Tenochtitlan, do you think they had brooms? James?
74. Student: (Indecipherable)
75. Teacher: Oh, the people went down the street and used brooms. We now have a great big machine that squirts water out and a big broom thing that goes around and around and

one man drives it. Would anyone like to add anything? OK, you had your hand up.

76. Student: (Indecipherable)
77. Teacher: (Indecipherable)
78. Student: (Indecipherable)
79. Teacher: OK. Selling (indecipherable). That's a good point. Some people have. . . . Do you know anyone who has a compost pile, big on gardening.
80. Student: (Indecipherable)
81. Teacher: They use a lot of wastes. They let it decompose, and they use it as a fertilizer. It makes good fertilizer. Now they even use the dumps. They fill those in. They dig great big holes in the ground and fill them in with garbage and eventually, when it's full, they cover it and all the garbage will decompose and it, it's good for the earth. It supplies a lot of nutrients for anything that grows, like grass (indecipherable), anything. OK. Would anyone like to add something? Does anyone have anything they would like to add? About the sanitation systems and what they share? OK. Number five. What were some other problems and how did they deal with them?
82. Student: (Indecipherable) people litter and gasses are in the air.
83. Teacher: That is correct.
84. Student: (Indecipherable)
85. Teacher: And overcrowding. That's a good point. There's overcrowding. Both cities had overcrowding and pollution. Erin?
86. Student: (Indecipherable, long answer)
87. Teacher: OK. Both cities had a problem with flooding. Like we said, we don't deal with them in the same way, but we both do try to deal with the, the problem. Tenochtitlan used dikes, while we use our sewer system, gutters, ditches, someplace for the water to run off. Theresa, what were you going to say?
88. Student: (Indecipherable)
89. Teacher: Flooding, what about flooding?
90. Student: (Indecipherable) air pollution (indecipherable).
91. Teacher: Pollution problems, population problems.
92. Student: (Indecipherable)
93. Teacher: Crime, crime was a problem for them too? How did they deal with it?
94. Student: (Indecipherable)
95. Teacher: I'm sorry, what?
96. Student: (Indecipherable)

97. Teacher: How does Houston deal with their crime problem?
98. Student: (Indecipherable)
99. Teacher: We've got jails. We both have systems of some type of police. People who enforce the law.
100. Student: (Indecipherable)
101. Teacher: Prevent crime.
102. Student: Sanitation problems (indecipherable).
103. Teacher: Once again the problem of sanitation. Both have street cleaners and garbage men, someone who is responsible for picking up all the garbage and disposing of it. OK. Let's look at number six. "Is the level of technology in the two cities similar?" And explain your answer.
104. Student: Yes. Both have (indecipherable) and people who help the sick.
105. Teacher: OK. And the (indecipherable) was the same. But the Aztecs did have doctors to care for the people. They tried to be more scientific about it. They weren't just voodoo, witch doctors, and things like that. They may not have been as good as the doctors we have today, like the doctors we will have twenty years from now may be even better than the doctors we have today. But they did have doctors. Stan?
106. Student: (Indecipherable)
107. Teacher: Yes and no. Yes, there were a lot of similarities, but of course, we have had, we've had four and a half centuries to learn. We are more modern. Our level of technology is probably higher. Sean?
108. Student: (Indecipherable)
109. Teacher: That's correct. They didn't have the machinery that we have, but they did have some level of technology. Pam?
110. Student: (Indecipherable, long answer)
111. Teacher: Yes, it was very advanced for a city in the sixteenth century. So they, they may not have been as advanced as we are, but they did have. . . . They were not, they were not as we often think of people who lived long ago. They were not know-nothings who didn't know how to take care of themselves or take care of other people. George, were you going to say something?
112. Student: They both had a high level of technology and they both, both built buildings and traded things.
113. Teacher: They had a system of trade. They had a type of economy, um hum. They built buildings. They constructed things, um hum. Would anyone like to add anything? To any of the questions? OK. First, I need to take up these questions, then go back to our original seats. Be sure your name is on them, everyone's name in the group. . . .

Pattern	Data	Intended/Incidental Learning
Teacher repeats student.	5,7,9,13,15,21,23(?),25, 27,31,34,36,50,52,54, 60,64(?),66,68,70,73, 79,85,87,91,93,99,109, 111,113	Reinforcement for group benefit, as individuals tended to talk softly. Gives credence to an individual's answer.
Elaborates on student's answer.	7,13,19,21,31,34,50,52, 54,58,64,75,81,87,103, 105,107,111	Reinforces lessons learned previously, one of the teacher's objectives for this lesson.
Answers student's question.	23(?),40,46,64(?),75,81, 101,107(?)	Limits thought process. Might be good to let another student answer.
Seeks one-word response.	42,46,52,56	Limits thought process.
Seeks yes/no response.	3,5,9,15,36,42,70,73,79	Again limits thought.
Corrects student response.	46,62,107	Done in a calm, positive manner, thus tends to clarify student thinking rather than putting student down.
Asks for elaboration/ specification.	11,89,93,95,97 11,25	Calls for broader/deeper thinking.
Positive reinforcement. "That's a good point." "That's correct."	15,34,79,85 21,58,60,83,109	Gives student feeling of self-satisfaction. More apt to answer if feels has something of value to say.
Seeks further remarks from the group.	7,13,19,34,38,75,81,113	May allow students to feel accepted, less inhibited about answering.
Open to student- initiated input.	51,54,58,103,105,109	May increase students' self-confidence in answering.
Makes sure student who wants to participate gets the chance.	87,111	Again, increases students' feeling of self-worth.

Pattern	Data	Intended/Incidental Learning
Asks for more response before moving on.	19,34,81	May increase students' feeling that their input is indeed valued, that the discussion is on their terms as well as the teacher's.
Asks for student to repeat answer.	48,56,89,95	Teacher, evidently, could not hear the student any better than the tape!
Keeps order. Invites all students to take part.	1,75 1,34	Teaches consideration for others. Students know they may participate, but must do so in an orderly way. May decrease spontaneity.
Calls for attention.	29,68	Because she makes "controlling" comments infrequently, students are more apt to pay attention to them.
Allows students to reply to each other.	32,33	Infrequency of student attempts to discuss the answers among selves may have been function of earlier small group activity.

INDEX